# VALUABLE

*We dedicate this book to all African women, because
you are our source of inspiration.*

# VALUABLE

*Discovering the Biblical Message through*
*the Eyes of African Women*

———

Copyright © 2022  / All Rights Reserved
Laura Gast, Natascha de Goey *&* Renalda Dijkhuizen

———



———

**ISBN:  978-90-79516-10-0**

———

**Foundation Press**
P.O. Box 12429 • 1100 AK Amsterdam
The Netherlands
apa.eu.com

———

**Layout & Design**
timmyroland.com

# VALUABLE

*Discovering the Biblical Message through
the Eyes of African Women*

# CONTENT

# Valuable

# INTRODUCTION

Congratulations, with this book you have a rich treasure in your hands! Valuable uncovers the stories of women in the Bible. We will explore their hardships and the lessons they have learned. And in this all we will discover that their lives, as well as their problems, challenges, and victories, are similar to ours. Their feelings of rejection, failure, doubt, or pain resemble our feelings and pain. We will find that God had a purpose with all of them. They played their part in the story of God's mission in this world. And, like us, these women were not always aware of this. Also, we as female followers of Jesus in Africa, are encouraged by God to play our part in his bigger story. And as they sometimes failed to see what God was doing in their lives, so do we. However, the stories in the Bible show us the bigger picture. The Spirit of God is at work from the creation of the earth till the day Jesus will make all things new.

It was a mighty Spirit that created the world. Did you know that spirit is a female word in the Bible? God is either male or female but exceeds both. So, although we refer to him as male, the way he creates, like a hen who broods on her eggs, or the way he cares, like a mother who cannot forget her children, relates also to the work of a woman. The Almighty One is above gender, and so much more than male or female.

Valuable

In the beginning, when the earth was made, the Spirit created all animals in pairs, but not Adam (Adam means earth or dirt and is the figure who represents all humans coming forth out of the earth). God created Adam in his image and as God, he carried the male and female parts within himself. But he was lonely and longed for a company other than the Almighty or the animals. God divided the male and female parts in him and created Eve, so the story goes. Eve is the mother of all living humans, which is why her name means: life, and in this way, she collaborates with God in creating humankind.

The sad part is that Adam and Eve disregarded the instructions of the Almighty and he banned them from this perfect and peaceful place called Eden. And this is where, in the Bible, the history of humankind on earth begins. Life becomes a struggle and conflicts, hunger, hardships find their way into the communities and hearts of the people. The Bible describes this in big steps from Genesis 1-11 and focuses from Genesis 12 on a man named Abram, who will be Abraham, the father of many peoples. In the New Testament, Jesus calls him the father of all believers. And in this way, Abraham is also our ancestor.

In this book, we read about Sarah and Hagar, the mothers of Abrahams's sons and the birth of the people of Israel but also of the Arabs, who descend from the line of Ismael. Through the eyes of women in the Bible, we will observe the hardship of Hagar and the destructive feelings of inferiority of Sarah. Subsequently, we read about the courage of Jochebed, the mother of the greatest Old Testament prophet Moses and the commitment of Ruth, one of the foremothers of King David and Jesus himself.

—

Moving towards the New Testament, the story of the children of Abraham continues. Throughout the whole Old Testament, the prophets promised that one day a Messiah, a Savior, would come to set the people of Israel free. He would be a King like David and a Deliverer like Moses, royal and powerful. What a surprise that God chooses a young and unimportant girl, Mary, to bring forth such a Redeemer. Just like Eve in the garden of Eden, Mary is the one who will bring forth life and carries the promise of the Spirit of God. It is an old prophetess who confirms that this baby Jesus will deliver Israel, not only from sin but also from the difficult mission in God's overarching plan to bring back humanity into his presence. Anna is in the temple when baby Jesus is dedicated by his parents to God, and she praises God for him.

When Jesus moved around to instruct the people about God, women play an important part. Two famous female followers were the sisters Mary and Martha who loved Jesus dearly as he loved them.

Jesus shows his love for the broken, the lonely, and the outcast when he heals a woman who suffers from losing blood for years. She is not only ill but also an outcast and impure. This way Jesus shows that although his ancestors were kings and he descended from heaven, his eyes are on the simple, poor, lonely, and sick people, on men and women alike. He came to heal our wounds and to show us a brighter future. And this is what he still wants to do in our lives.

We wrote and translated this book especially for women in Africa. Hagar is one of the first women in the Bible who had an encounter with God. And she is an African woman. She identifies God as the One who hears and sees. This is

—

our mission with this book: God sees you and hears your cries, doubts, questions, and complaints. This book is meant to encourage and comfort you.

We thank all who collaborated with us to make this happen and pray God's blessing over you.

Your sisters in Christ,

**Laura, Natascha *&* Renalda**

# VALUABE

*Discovering the Biblical Message through
the Eyes of African Women*

## LAURA GAST, NATASCHA DE GOEY
## & RENALDA DIJKHUIZEN

Foundation Press

# VALUABLE

# Eve

## BIBLE STORY

Eve enjoys her walks through the forest together with her spouse Adam. Every day she marvels at the beauty her Creator has made. So many beautiful things, she can hardly grasp them. Tall green trees, shrubs in all shapes and sizes with the most delicious juicy fruits for them to enjoy every single day. Flowers so colourful which no one could have imagined. She discovers new species every day. Even this morning: "Adam, look over there. Look how beautiful!" A field full of purple, yellow, and red flowers is shining in the morning sun.

Unexpectedly she is standing eye to eye with one of her dear friends, Mr Elephant. He hammers on her head with his big trunk. "Good morning to you too, Mr Elephant. You did not know this, but from now on that will be your name, personally given to you by Adam." They happily walk on enjoying all the sounds of the forest. This is Paradise. Full of vibrant life. Full of beauty, joy, and peace.

Suddenly a feeling of unrest comes over Eve. She does not understand where this comes from. She looks around but does not see anything unusual. Other than some trees she has not seen before, things appear normal. One of the trees bears enormous, delicious-looking fruits. She can hardly take her eyes off them; she looks fascinated at the deep orange and red fruits. She feels restless and wants to continue walking, could these fruits be the cause of this feeling? Surely this does not feel right. After all, this is the tree her Creator told her to stay away from. She does not understand, where this strange feeling comes from. This is not something she is familiar with.

Where did Adam go? He is no longer with her. Then suddenly she hears a voice. "Hello there, isn't this tree beautiful?" This is not Adam's voice; on the contrary, it seems to be coming from the ground. She looks down and she immediately feels growing anxiety within her. Sneaky eyes in a long stretchy body stare at her. "Is not that a nice tree?" the creepy creature says. Eve swallows, yes indeed. She steps back. She feels that she must leave. Yet, she does not, because in a way this also seems very exciting. Finally, someone who approaches her personally, and who gives her the attention she is longing for. She enjoys the attention this creature gives her even though he is as ugly as can be.

"Would you like to taste them?" "Well, no", she answers reluctantly, "my Creator would rather not let me do that. The fruits are not good for me, because they will cause death". The ugly creature looks at her in surprise. "Does your Creator say that? That is nonsense. You will not die from eating this fruit, it will make you very smart. You no longer have to listen to that Creator of yours, because you will get to know the difference between right and wrong, which makes you more powerful."

Eve has her doubts, of course, it sounds good, but is it true? Then she no longer must listen to others but can decide for herself what is right and wrong. She takes another look at the colourful fruits. What would they taste like? Sweet? Juicy? It makes her mouth water. Well, alright then, a small bite will not make a difference. She should taste together with Adam. He also must be part of it. She calls her husband and together they pick one of the fruits. The ugly creature watches them satisfactorily from below with his sneaky eyes and thinks: "This is going well. It is going very well!"

Eve bites into the juicy fruit they picked. Before she even swallows it, she already feels something has changed. What is this? She looks at Adam and suddenly a strange feeling comes over her. She cannot define it. She realizes her nakedness and feels the urge to cover herself. Her body no longer feels familiar. What about Adam? Does he feel the same? He does not even dare to look at her anymore. Sadness and despair overwhelm them; feelings they were not aware of before.

Suddenly they hear their Creator calling: "Adam? Eve? Where are you?" She is shocked; this is another feeling that she doesn't understand. She hides behind a bush, away from her Creator. The one who lovingly gives them everything they need. What will he say? Would he be angry and disappointed? Fear and shame, feelings she never felt before creeping, upon her. Completely confused, she wonders how this will ever work out between her and her Creator.

*Narrated from Genesis chapters 2 & 3*

## DISCUSSION

We all know that feeling when we do something we know is not the right thing to do. And, just like Eve, we sometimes do ignore these feelings and go ahead anyway.

◊	Why do you think that is?

◊   Would there be a way to stop following this voice in your head telling you to do things that are not right?

After both Adam and Eve ate from the forbidden fruit they feel ashamed and hide from their Creator.

◊   What does their Creator do?

◊   Though their relationship has drastically changed he is still looking for their companionship. What does that say about our Creator, our God?

◊   Can the relationship with God be restored?

## LIFE EXPERIENCE

Latifa is a young woman who just turned sixteen. She likes to explore the world. However, she is the last born in a family with 3 elder brothers. As the only female sibling, she must do most of the daily chores in the compound. Her father is financially able to send her to school, which allowed her to learn more about life outside the village where she was brought up. One day she went to school, and she decided to stay behind with some friends for a drink before going back to the compound. When she came home she was late for cooking. Her brothers were not happy that she came home late, because now they had to wait for their food. So, they decided to punish her. They beat her mercilessly with a cane. Not only on her legs but also her head and back were hit with it. Simply because she came home later than she was supposed to.

When I heard the story, many of my friends supported the behaviour of the girl's brothers. They argued that the girl did not obey her duties and therefore she needed to be punished. I think it was too harsh to punish the girl so severely just for coming home late. Though she made a mistake by forsaking her duties in the compound, she did not deserve such a severe beating.

When Eve ate from the fruit which was forbidden she also received a punishment. After God cursed the serpent, he cursed both Eve and Adam. To Eve he said that he would increase her trouble in pregnancy and double the pain when giving birth, despite all that she would still long for her husband, but he will surely rule over her (Gen. 3:16). This curse was given to Eve, and since she represents all women the curse affects all future women. The same applies to Adam. He represents all men, which means that all men will rule over their wives. Or as some see it; men will rule over women. However, despite God cursing both the serpent, Adam, and Eve, he also gave them a future promise! We will explore this further in our Bible study. Though he cast them out of Paradise, he still seeks their companionship, and he continues to help them throughout their lives on earth.

What does this story teach us? Does it teach us that whenever we disobey God, that he will punish us? Does it teach us that whenever we disobey our family or friends or religious leaders we should receive punishment? Or is God merciful and would he show compassion? And should we follow his example and be merciful to one another?

We know God to be a merciful God. He is our Redeemer. Whenever we do something which is not good for us he can deliver us from that. We can always turn to him in prayer and confess that we took a wrong turn in life, and he will help us through it. This is also how God wants us to treat one another. Jesus teaches us that whenever someone is wronging us we should forgive him seven times seven times.

Being forgiven or forgiving others does not undo the consequences of our life's choices, but it helps us to reunite with our neighbours and to reunite with God and accept his companionship.

He wants to make things right between you and him and therefore he continuously gives us grace.

## DISCUSSION

- ◈ How can God help release you from these troubles, undo the curse?
- ◈ What do you think would be your role within God's plan to save others from punishment?
- ◈ How could we be more merciful to our family, friends, and neighbours?

## BIBLE STUDY

*Though I walk amid trouble, you preserve my life; you stretch out your hand against the wrath of my enemies, and your right hand delivers me. The Lord will fulfil his purpose for me; your steadfast love, O Lord, endures forever. Do not forsake the work of your hands. Psalm 138:7-8 (ESV)*

Eve, which means 'life' or 'mother of all living' is created by God with a purpose, perfectly and with much attention and love. Together with Adam, she is assigned to take care of and inhabit the world which God created. What an honour and what a huge present!

God very consciously chooses her. A new creation who can give life, and who matches perfectly with Adam. How happy and grateful he is. God has given him an equal partner to share everything with. Together with God, as a family, they take care of the earth in perfect joy and harmony. This is God's plan.

Unfortunately, things go wrong. Eve is seduced. She cannot resist eating from the forbidden tree because of the promise to become just as smart as her Creator.

Temptation: we can all relate to it. Persuading someone to do something they do not want to do or are not allowed to do. Or being persuaded to do something that is not good for you and yet you cannot resist it. There are so many temptations. For instance, when we want something and we cannot get it, we might do anything that lies within our power to get hold of it. You know it is not right, and yet you cannot stop yourself. And before you know it, you are in trouble. This is exactly how it was for Eve. The desire to taste these beautiful fruits and the idea to become smarter than her Creator are too much for her to resist. However, her decision has huge consequences.

Immediately thereafter her relationship with Adam and her Creator changes. The perfect love and harmony turn into reproach, accusation, and an urge to dominate. Something we still experience up to this present day. We experience this within our family, among friends, and within our community. It has changed the whole world. Instead of seeing him as a loving God, we see him as a threat and that is exactly what the serpent wanted to achieve: separation. He succeeded to destroy the confidential and equal relationship between men and women and between humanity and God.

But God is the Champion. And to achieve victory, he consciously chooses Eve, an imperfect woman. God does not blame her, because of her womanhood. And he is not letting her down even though she made a mistake. Yes, she must leave Paradise, and yes, she also must bear the consequences for her mistake (Gen. 3:16). But through her, as the mother of all who are living, victory will be achieved over evil and the intimate relationship with God and humanity will be restored, eventually.

God curses the serpent (Gen.3:15). Within this curse lies an incredible promise for humankind in which Eve and every woman born after her would play an important role.

> *"I will make you and the woman hate each other; her offspring and yours will always be enemies. Her offspring will crush your head, and you will bite her offspring's heel." Gen 3:15 (GNT)*

This means so much as that life on earth will often be an agony. The serpent bits the heel of humankind. We will feel the pain, but it will not kill us. However, in the end, the one offspring of that woman will overcome the serpent by crushing its head which will eliminate him.

Many generations later, that promise to humankind is partly fulfilled. God chooses a descendant of Eve, Mary, a humble village girl from Nazareth, to give birth to the saviour of mankind, Jesus Christ. And he will crush the serpent's head.

# DISCUSSION

We all know moments in our lives where we believe God is no longer present. He left us, or he no longer cares. We do not feel his presence, not even when we pray or when we are in church. Temptation or doubts can separate us from God and prevent us from having a relationship with him.

- ◈   What separates you from God?

- ◈   And how do you think this gap between God and you can be reduced?

- ◈   How do you cope with the suffering that life brings? Is the promise of God to Eve help you get through these hardships?

## IN-DEPTH STUDY (for leaders)

*I have called you by name. Isaiah 43:1c*

Receiving a name at birth is important! A name shows that you have the right to exist. You are someone. You are allowed to take your place in the world.

Names were essential in biblical times. Names have meaning; they tell a story. And therefore, names are given with a purpose. It does not have to be a fancy name, but it tells something about the circumstances in which the child was born and indicates something about the temperament of the baby and the expectations for the child.

This is still very common here in Africa. For example, the meaning of the name Akyiremu is so much as: 'has kept too long' This name can be given to a child who likes it very much inside his mother's womb and does not want to come out at the right time. Moreover, the name might also bring expectations and hope with it. The female name Hope is very popular for that reason.

Earlier we said that Eve means 'life' or 'to give life' but the name is also interpreted as being the mother of all living. She is the first woman on earth and thus she also becomes the first mother of children but her name has a much deeper meaning. Adam confirms God's promise with this new name. Through her a Messiah, Saviour, Rescuer will be born, and he will crush the head of the serpent. He will conquer the enemy, the adversary. That is why the name Eve is a hopeful forward-looking name at those times. And it still is, because the name Eve also implies that she had the right to live. And as the mother of all living, she passes on this life to other women.

Therefore, name-giving is a very important event, it reveals the character or a trait of that person. A very beautiful example is God's name. The Bible mentions more than a hundred names and all those names reveal something about his character, about who he is! Such as Comforter, Helper, Counsellor, Rock, Healer, Eternal One, and Breath of Life.

God blew his Breath of Life into Adam and Eve, which is how they came to life. He created them in his image. Full of life and full of love. God gave us the power to pass on this life and love to others. And this goes further than bearing children. God gave us his creativity and divine power so that we can express this love in many ways. We share this love by caring for one another and by caring for everything he created on earth. By preparing a lovely meal, weaving a beautiful cloth, or listening to people who are in pain and sorrow. Love is also being able to forgive people who have hurt us. In short, there are countless ways to share your love received from God.

In addition, God decided to share his spirit with us, which enables us to love him, hear his voice, and receive his wisdom. In this way, we get to know him and follow him more and more. In this way, we discover the desire in ourselves to share his love.

Another beautiful name of God is the name by which he introduces himself to Moses. Moses is commissioned by God to lead the people out of Egypt, but Moses wondered how he was going to tell this to the people. Who is it that gives me this assignment? How am I supposed to call you?

And then God says: Just say my name: I AM. I am the One who is and always will be.

'Breath of Life' and 'I Am' are the two most meaningful names of God. They fit together beautifully, for with his Breath of Life he has consciously chosen to give us life and by connecting his name 'I Am' to it, he promises us that he will always be there and that he will not forsake us.

# VALUABLE

## TIPS

1. Watch this short inspiring video.
   https://youtu.be/PbREmRdjvTc

2. The Presence project has inspiring messages for us about God's presence. Personally, this poem touched me deeply. Read the poem and be inspired!

*Oh God my God*

*how little I comprehend Your being.*

*My vision is misted over*

*a dense fog lies between us.*

*I see only the faintest ray of Your vast sun.*

*Your magnitude is hidden from my earthly eyes.*

*Your glory I only know in part.*

*I truly fail to grasp You fully.*

*Understanding lies perpetually beyond my reach.*

*How I long for the day of our meeting*

*To finally see you without human hindrance.*

*Then I will be able to praise You more truly.*

https://youtu.be/J4BpEl4SPV4

3.  Listen to this song and sing along if you know the  words. By doing so try to listen with your heart and let the Holy Spirit touch you. Every verse has a promise and a message. Which promise is most important for you? Think about all the messages you have heard in the song. How do you think to put one or more of these into practice within your own life?

https://youtu.be/I0R35mVzftE

# VALUABLE

# SARAH

## BIBLE STORY

Sarah looks at young Ishmael as he returns from a walk with Abraham. Her stomach tightens as it usually does when she sees them together. She sees how her husband turns his face lovingly to Ishmael and how he intensively listens to what his son is telling him. Sarah continues her activities; it is just the way it is. She is too old to have another child and Ishmael has become Abraham's pride and his only descendant.

How different Sarah had imagined it. From the moment she left her mother's house with Abraham, she longed to have a son. Abraham even believes that the Almighty promised him one, but Sarah does not believe that. Why would the Almighty speak to her husband? He is not such a sweetheart, as his wife, she knows all about that.

When the Almighty spoke to him for the first time, Sarah and Abraham were very enthusiastic about this promise. As the years went by, she increasingly doubts if Abraham has not just imagined his meeting with the Almighty. That is also the reason why she suggested that Abraham should sleep with her slave girl Hagar. At least then there will be a child and Sarah hoped to find peace of mind. Why should she not take matters into her own hands to provide offspring, since the Almighty seems not to care about her?

Sarah is tired of life; she is tired of the hard life as a nomad, and she is tired of competing with her Egyptian slave girl. She had so hoped that Abraham's son would be her son too. She insisted that she would teach Ishmael the basics of life. Despite him being in her presence during his early childhood, his eyes do not twinkle the way they do when he sees his mother Hagar, and he only wants to sleep in her tent. Every day Sarah feels rejected; several times she considered sending Hagar away and keeping Ishmael with her. However, her inner voice tells her not to do so.

Visitors are coming. She sees three men walking towards Abraham who is resting under the big tree. With her hand above her eyes, she peers into the distance to see if she recognizes these men. She sends one of the servants to find out about the purpose of this visit. He returns together with Abraham and tells her that the men need water to wash their feet and that they are hungry and would like to eat under the tree. It is an important visit since the fattened calf is brought to be slaughtered.

Abraham provides seats and Sarah follows him with water to wash the men's feet. She looks at them closely as she wipes their feet with a cloth. No, it is not a family visit, but one of the men does look very familiar. That man watches her thoughtfully, but when their eyes meet, Sarah looks away shyly.

When Sarah, together with some servants, eventually serves the meal it has already become dark. The men sit comfortably around the fire and Sarah offers them the opportunity to wash their hands before they eat. Then the baskets of food are placed in the centre. The servants go back into their tents, but Sarah stays within hearing distance in

—

case the men need anything else.

Startled, Sara suddenly hears her name. The same man who looked at her before, now asks where she is. When he continues Sarah hears him say, "I will come back to you in exactly one year and then your wife Sarah will have a son". Sarah laughs unintentionally and thinks to herself, this is not possible at all, is it? She was not intimate with Abraham for many years and they are both too old to have children. Sunk away in her thoughts, she notices the man talking about her again. "Why is your wife laughing?", he asks Abraham. "Is anything too difficult for the Almighty?" Sarah blushes and she mutters, "I did not laugh," although she and the man know better.

That night, Sarah is not able to fall asleep. Repeatedly she hears the words of the man saying that by next year she will have a son. Would it finally happen after all those years? A little hope arises in her heart, but her disbelief beats the hope. Certainly, it is not possible; she did not have her period for years. How could she ever have a child? Did not the man say that nothing is too hard for the Almighty though? Finally, Sarah dozes off with a little smile on her face.

*Narrated from Genesis 18:1-15*

## DISCUSSION

◊   Is there something that you have long been waiting for that you believe God wants to give to you but is not coming?

◊   How does this affect you, and your faith?

◊   How do you fill or spend this (waiting) time?

## LIFE EXPERIENCE

Having offspring is very important in our culture. There can be a lot of peer pressure and if a child is not expected within one year of marriage, the pressure might soon be exerted on the man to take a second wife. This happens amongst all of us, both Muslims and Christians. Providing offspring is a high priority. This concerns Mary Y. very much. She is a young Dagomba girl in her early twenties and recently married. She and her husband had a church marriage and they have put their trust in God. Just a few months earlier her husband's brother also got married and his wife was pregnant within weeks. As culture dictates, the brothers still live in the same compound with the rest of the family, and Mary is confronted every day with the fact that her sister-in-law gave birth to a baby girl, and she has not been pregnant yet. She puts her hope in God, but at the same time, she is deeply concerned, because she knows that if she does not conceive within a year, she must share her husband with another woman. Even though her husband does not particularly want this, it is expected of him. Mary is so worried about this that she is struggling to enjoy her marriage.

Every week she is prayed for and even though she says she is very grateful for this, somewhere deep inside it feels unfair, and she struggles with her desires and her fears. Do the promises from the Bible not apply to her? There are obstacles she is unaware of? Doesn't she have enough faith? Questions anyone with an unfulfilled desire will ask as they seek healing or relief through prayer. Questions that are not easy to answer and to which no general answer could and should be given.

**Struggling with God**

We all struggle with unfulfilled desires. Illness, the loss of a loved one, not being able to have children, finding the right partner, or a job. All these life events have a major impact on our lives if they do not happen as we expect them to. However, when struggling one always has a choice: do you become a bitter or a better person? Is it possible to experience peace of mind about the situation in which you are struggling? I think it is possible, but not without a fight. It makes a huge difference with Whom you fight, though!

# DISCUSSION

◊    Is it okay to wrestle with God?

◊    Isn't that disrespectful, isn't it just better to accept what he has to offer you in this life? How do you see this? Discuss it with each other.

# BIBLE STUDY

*Hope deferred makes the heart sick, but a desire fulfilled is a tree of life. Proverbs 13:12 (ESV)*

While the Book of Proverbs regularly appeals to 'common sense', this verse focuses on the heart. The heart is pictured as the centre of our emotions, our deliberations, the basis of our emotional life. Although there is often a rational explanation for an unfulfilled desire, such as lack of finances for expensive fertility treatment, or to make a trip to a faraway relative, the heart usually does not go along with our reasoning. Our mind is complicated, and the writer of Proverbs understands this.

This verse also shows that an unfulfilled desire can be very real and has a great impact on our lives. It can make our hearts sick. It is often the case that physical complaints follow psychological or spiritual problems. We can become sick due to sadness.

Furthermore, this verse says that a fulfilled desire not only brings joy but is a tree of life. This is reminiscent of the tree in paradise and represents full life. Life as originally intended! Not only joy in the form of a happy feeling, but our whole being is part of it. Living according to body, soul, and spirit.

This contains more than the desire for a job, a child, or someone we miss terribly. If these are fulfilled, for example, an answered prayer or a surprise visit from that faraway relative, we will certainly be happy, and it will have a positive impact on our well-being. Does that mean we are full of life then? I doubt that because what if our earthly desire is not fulfilled? For instance, when we are not healed from a disease or when we do not have children, does this mean we are not a part of this tree of life?

## DISCUSSION

What is the condition for a happy and fruitful life? When does life make sense? It is a simple question, but the answer ...

## IN-DEPTH STUDY (for leaders)

*Every one of those people died. But they still had faith, even though they had not received what they had been promised. They were glad just to see these things from far away, and they agreed that they were only strangers and foreigners on this earth. When people talk this way, they are looking for a place to call their own. If they had been talking about the land where they had once lived, they could have gone back at any time. But they were looking forward to a better home in heaven. That is why God wasn't ashamed for them to call him their God. He even built a city for them. Hebrews 11:13-16*

Hebrews 11 shows us that not every God-fearing man or woman saw the desires or promises fulfilled during their lifetime. These heroes are listed in Hebrews 11 because of their faith, as an example for the Christian Jews of that time. The first verse strikingly says:

*Now faith is the assurance of things hoped for, the conviction of things not seen. (ESV)*

Faith and hope are thus linked together; they form a striking connection. The word hope implies that in addition to the expectation of something better here on earth, there is also the expectation of a better future. This word (hope) is always used about the future, a future in which the community of God is reflected. In the book of Hebrews, this is described as a better home in heaven. Something to look forward to when our desires are not (all) fulfilled. The combination with the word faith indicates an expectation of the coming of the Messiah who will make all things new. It is a certainty that this will happen, not a mirage or dream whose reality is not real.

## TIPS

1.    You usually know whether you have peace of mind about your unfulfilled desires or whether you are still struggling. With peace of mind, I do not mean that you

—

will never be sad about the situation again, but that you can accept God's greater plan. To evaluate this, you could thank God for your suffering. If you can do that, that is impressive, but if you are not able to, please do not worry. There won't be peace without a struggle. Try to pray the following prayer:

"Heavenly Father, I don't think it's fair that you didn't give me . . . (Fill in your heart's desire) . . . You know how I long for it and I know you can give it to me!

But when I think about it I realize that You did not give Jesus what he wanted either. When he prayed in Gethsemane, "O My Father, if it is possible, let this cup pass from Me" it did not happen. That was not fair, but he died for the greater plan! Please, Lord, help me to understand that there may be a greater plan and help me to accept it so that my suffering can play a part in the salvation of others. Thank you, Lord Jesus, for accepting your suffering, helping me to do the same. Please, show me the way forward so that my heart does not go weary and that I may live from the tree of life. And if this is not the right time, please let me be more patient and encourage me with Your words".

2.	Make a list of all your blessings. From my own experience, I know that when you are facing difficulties the more you can see every small blessing in your life. Consciously thank God for those little blessings because thanking God makes room for new blessings.

3.	The song Blessings by Laura Story gives more insights into the way God sometimes answers. Due to her husband's illness at a very young age, she had to adjust her future perspective. This song expresses her questions and her surrender:

https://youtu.be/XQan9L3yXjc

*We pray for blessings, we pray for peace*
*Comfort for family, protection while we sleep*
*We pray for healing, for prosperity*
*We pray for Your mighty hand to ease our suffering*
*And all the while, You hear each spoken need*
*Yet love us way too much to give us lesser things*

CHORUS:
*Cause what if Your blessings come through raindrops*
*What if Your healing comes through tears*
*What if a thousand sleepless nights are what it takes*
*to know You're near*
*What if trials of this life are Your mercies in disguise?*

*We pray for wisdom, Your voice to hear*
*And we cry in anger when we cannot feel You near*
*We doubt Your goodness, we doubt Your love*
*As if every promise from Your Word is not enough*
*And all the while, You hear each desperate plea*
*And long that we'd have faith to believe*

BRIDGE:

*When friends betray us*
*When darkness seems to win, we know*
*The pain reminds this hearts,*
*That this is not, this is not our home.....*
*It's not our home*

# VALUABLE

# VALUABLE

# HAGAR

## BIBLE STORY

Hagar proudly raises her head. No one will see her cry, never! She does not look back for a minute when she travels with her new mistress. Away from Egypt, far from her family and friends. Though life was not easy in Pharaoh's house, it was home to Hagar. With her head upright and her back straightened she is a striking appearance, but the look in her eyes prevents all other slaves from speaking to her. Even the children stay far away from her, so Hagar has plenty of time to nurture her hatred and pride during the trip to Canaan.

The slaves walk in front of the caravan with the camels, donkeys, and sheep. A piece of cattle, which is all she is, goes through Hagar's mind. Phew, she thought for a moment that the pharaoh himself liked her. All those days when she was set aside to be dressed up, to soften her sun-tanned skin with luscious oils, and to have her hair washed by the young girls with whom she first shared the women's quarters. Yes, she thought she was being prepared to become Pharaoh's mistress.

Her disappointment was enormous when it turned out that she was to be a present. Not for Pharaoh, though. No, she was meant for a woman from another country that Pharaoh had somehow fallen in love with. She was simply given away, not even sold for a high price. She was led into the courtyard with all kinds of camels, donkeys, and a large herd of cattle. "This is for you and your brother," Pharaoh said to the beautiful lady he liked so much. "You can do whatever you want with it. Only the best for my most beautiful!"

For a few months, she is the personal caretaker of Pharaoh's new love. Now she understands why she had to undergo a beauty treatment herself. One cannot wash a woman's body with rough hands, right? Then one would not only scrub the dead cells off the skin but the entire skin itself! Some days Hagar wished she could do so since her new mistress does not pay any attention to her at all. No kind word is given to Hagar, and she is ignored completely by her new mistress. Had Hagar not been so full of her feelings, she would have noticed that her mistress was paying no attention to anyone because she has been very unhappy all this time. Hagar is too busy with herself to notice that.

One day the mistress comes running into her rooms. "Let's go, quickly", she shouts, "pack everything, collect all my things. We have to get out of here before the sun goes down". Hagar does not understand what is going on, but she obediently packs everything and loads it onto the camels. Will she be allowed to stay here? In her home, in the neighbourhood, and close to her relatives? When the caravan leaves messily and hastily, she almost manages to get away unseen. Until a strong hand takes her and pushes her towards other slaves who are walking with the donkeys, she is expected to come along with them!

—

Hagar ponders about all this when she walks along with the caravan. It is almost dark now and they must start looking for a place to spend the night. Hagar considers her chances of fleeing, but she notices that Eliazer, the co-worker of her new master, is watching her closely. When they finally stop to set up their night camp, she feels the same firm hand around her arm. She is taken to her mistress. She is expected to arrange water and to start a fire. As if she had not walked for hours while her mistress sat comfortably on the donkey's back. Inwardly Hagar boils of anger, but she does not show anything about her feelings. She bottles up everything, hides her true feelings, and makes sure that no one sees what is going on inside her.

Ten years later, the situation has not changed much. Hagar still takes care of her mistress. Although the caravan regularly stays at the same place for a longer period, they live in tents. When Sarah, her mistress, is asleep, Hagar can go to the women's tent. Usually, she cannot sleep instantly but thinks a lot about the past. At first, she missed her family and the comforts of the city of the Pharaoh so much, the pleasant markets, the people, the language. This has all faded over the years though. She has not been able to accept any of it, but instead, she holds a grudge against Sarah. The rejections of recent years hardened her. The look on her face is even prouder and more distant.

Then, suddenly, Sarah comes to the women's tent. This is very exceptional and Hagar wonders whether she has forgotten something, but Sarah says, "Gather your things, I'm giving you to my husband." Hagar gasps because she understands what the intention is. It is not about her; it is about what she can produce as a woman. She must give a child to Abraham and Sarah since they are childless. Hagar swallows when she thinks about Abraham, who is at least fifty years older, but as usual, she says nothing and takes the little she owns in a cloth and leaves for the tents of her new master.

Within a month she is pregnant and despite all the grudges she has toward her mistress, something happens inside Hagar: pride! She can do something her mistress failed to do. Now, Hagar feels superior to Sarah, and she is taking advantage of the situation. She is increasingly ignoring her orders and she lies lazily on her bed because she is supposedly sick. Sarah becomes angry and says to Abraham: "Now look how that slave of yours treats me just because she got pregnant!" Sarah is furious with Abraham, but Abraham says, "I give her back to you, do what you want with her!" Sarah acts fast and before Hagar realizes what is happening, she receives ten lashes for her disobedience and is banished again to the women's tent of the slaves.

That night Hagar packs her things and decides to flee. She wants to get out of there forever! Even if this would kill her! This life is so unfair, so unfair she thinks.

*Narrated from Genesis 16*

## DISCUSSION

◊    Do you recognize yourself in her?

◊    Is there a situation in your life where you had the same kind of feeling? The feeling of being unseen and maltreated?

◊    Do you think life is fair? How do you cope with that?

# LIFE EXPERIENCE

When Aida was a young girl, in her teenage years, she stayed at the house of an uncle and aunt in Zambia for quite some months. There was also a cousin in the house, a few years older than her. He started to visit her at night, the first night they only chatted, but the second he tried to kiss her. Aida did not know what to do, it was not something she wanted to happen. She talked to her uncle and aunt, and they said: you need to endure this. He is family, it is not a big deal. So it happened that he slept with her, and Aida could do nothing about it. She did not talk about this for over twenty years because she was so ashamed. When she finally dared to share her story, she found out that many of her friends shared the same experience of being raped by family members. It seems so unfair that young girls have no control over their lives and that a big thing like having a sexual relationship is dismissed as something irrelevant.

**Fatalism or prosperity**

It depends on our background how we deal with questions like: Why is this happening to me, why is God not doing anything? Some people think that God allows it and so we must accept it as his will. Then they accept the difficulties and suffering in their lives. They often think that God will have a purpose for it and that we must, therefore (patiently) undergo it. On the other hand, some people think that God will always intervene. They believe we must fight all suffering, illness, and adversity through prayer and fasting. If the suffering does not go away, then there must be something wrong with our faith and they wonder why the grace of God is not reaching us. However, the question is not: WHY is

God not doing anything? Or why is this happening to me?", but rather, "WHERE is God in this situation?"

That is the same question Jesus asked when he was about to die: "My God, my God, why have you forsaken me?" WHERE are you? It screams through this lonely and inhuman suffering. Was there ever anything more unfair than the death of this innocent man who gave his life for humanity? He suffered in loneliness; his friends even fell asleep. He died abandoned by God, or so it seems. However, he endured this horrific suffering so that you and I do not have to go through anything without him anymore.

## DISCUSSION

◇    Have you experienced the situation which is described by Aida?

◇    How do you react when you face obstacles in your life? Do you consider this as God's will for you, or do you argue and struggle with him about your problem? Is that appropriate?

◇    Have you ever cried out to God: Where are you, Lord? How did that feel? Did it bring you closer to a solution to your problem?

## BIBLE STUDY

*So, she called the name of the Lord who spoke to her, "You are a God of seeing", for she said, "Truly here I have seen him who looks after me." Genesis 16:13 (ESV)*

Hagar's story does not end with her flight into the desert. In Genesis 16 we read that an angel sees Hagar and speaks to her, "Where are you from and where are you going?" A question that shows interest and insight. The answer to this question is not that simple. She fled from a difficult situation, but where would she go now?

I do not think the angel's response is what Hagar hopes to hear. He says that she must go back to Sarah and endure the situation. This is very much against our sense of justice, but at the same time, it shows that it is not God's intention to change Hagar's difficult circumstances. You better just go back into slavery and the hopelessness, which is not what we would like to hear from an almighty God! Do we?

Yet Hagar benefits from this meeting because from her exclamation we learn that she has discovered that she is not alone in her difficult circumstances. God sees her! He turns to her and finds her, an Egyptian slave woman, worthwhile to send an angel to and to speak to her. To be seen, a world of difference!

In addition, the angel gives Hagar a promise, a glimpse into the future. The Lord has not only seen her, but he has also heard her. There is a future ahead of them!

Hagar has also seen herself. She has met the living God, and she even gave him a name: El Roi; the living One who sees me. God came closer to her, and she has gotten to know him better. The God of Abraham has now become her God as well. Being with him is very different from being alone with her anger, sadness, and loneliness.

—

Meeting the God who sees and hears everything makes all the difference! Not everything has changed immediately, but being seen, no longer standing alone, and looking ahead to the future. That is our heavenly Father, our God who wants to continue working in and through us.

## DISCUSSION

◈    How can you be sure that God is close
     in every situation?

◈    What does this do to you, does it guide you?

◈    Or do you experience God is unreachable for you?
     How do you cope with that?

## IN-DEPTH STUDY (for leaders)

The angel finds Hagar at the water source, a place where life springs up from the ground. Here, at this place, Hagar can rest from her escape from Abrahams's tents. She stopped for a moment so that there is time and opportunity for an encounter with God through a messenger, the angel. Significant is the name which Hagar gives to the source or the well: Lachai Roi, herein lies the words life and see. These two are linked together at the source! There is a lesson to be learned here, a lesson which Jesus repeats when he meets the woman from Samaria at the well. Here too it concerns a woman who is broken through life. Jesus shows that he knows her in and out, just like the angel with Hagar. Then these words follow:

—

*"Everyone who drinks this water will get thirsty again. But no one who drinks the water I give will ever be thirsty again. The water I give is like a flowing fountain that gives eternal life." (John 4:13-14)*

A well in a town is a meeting place, a place of exchange, of life. A place where God sees you and wants to fill you with hope, with recognition, with love, with his presence. Hagar, the Samaritan woman, you, and me, we must go up to that well where we can find him. We are invited to drink that living water that cleanses us and never makes us thirsty again. In this way, we will also become a source for others who need such an encounter. God sees Hagar, Jesus sees the Samaritan woman, who do we see?

## TIPS

1.    A sorrow shared is a sorrow halved is a common proverb. Being able to share one's suffering and receive understanding makes the suffering more bearable and alleviates distress. If sorrows cannot be shared, suffering may increase. Find a sister or a friend who is also going through a difficult time and share your sorrows. It will help to lift yourself and may help you to overcome the difficulties you are facing.

2.    Read the following poem and think about the message that the author wants to share with us:

**Footprints In the Sand**

One night a man had a dream. He dreamed.
he was walking along the beach with the LORD.

Across the sky flashed scenes from his life.
For each scene he noticed two sets of
footprints in the sand: one belonging.
to him, and the other to the LORD.
When the last scene of his life flashed before him,
he looked back at the footprints in the sand.

He noticed that many times along the path of
his life there was only one set of footprints.

He also noticed that it happened at the very.
lowest and saddest times in his life.

This bothered him and he
questioned the LORD about it:

"LORD, you said that once I decided to follow.
you, you would walk with me all the way.
But I have noticed that during the most.
troublesome times in my life,
there is only one set of footprints.
I don't understand why when.
I needed you most you would leave me."

The LORD replied:

"My son, my precious child,
I love you and I would never leave you.
During your times of trial and suffering,
when you see only one set of footprints,
it was then that I carried you."

*Author / Carolyn Joyce Carty*

https://youtu.be/8fuUY-N0ipk 

# VALUABLE

# JOCHEBED

## BIBLE STORY

Worried, Jochebed looks up to her husband. "I do hope it's a girl this time," she sighs as she places her hand protectively on her belly. Normally, Amram would disagree with her, because boys are more important to the family heir than girls, but this time he nods thoughtfully. Little Aaron and Miriam sense the mood and look at them with eyes wide open. Jochebed would have liked to give them both a carefree childhood, but the political situation in the land of the great river is becoming more and more difficult for her people. The men are put to work from early morning until late at night to help build the great city of the kings. The women are doing their best and are barely surviving. There is so much pressure from Pharaoh's army! Soldiers harass them as they come unexpectedly to check if there are pregnant women amongst them. Young girls are not safe as they are easy prey for the eager soldiers. Therefore, the women always group and do not let anyone go to the river alone for fetching water or washing clothes. Aaron is too young to understand the seriousness of the situation. His birth alone was a miracle. It was just before Pharaoh ordered the soldiers to drown all newborn boys.

—

Jochebed smiles inwardly when she thinks of her friend Shiphrah who helped her deliver. She silently came in the middle of the night, so no soldier could hear her. She helped to deliver the baby as she did with so many women in their neighbourhood, but she disappeared before dawn. Later in the day she had come back to discover that the child had been born already shouting out loud for every soldier to hear, "how is this possible? Have you already finished giving birth? Did I miss it again!" Every time she made sure that a passing soldier would hear her. At first, Jochebed did not understand the reason for this charade, but then Shiphrah explained to her that she was ordered to kill the Hebrew boys at birth. If it were clear that she had not been present at the delivery, she could not fulfil this commandment. She wanted to obey the Almighty God and he blessed her for it since she had many children of her own.

Once again, the laws have been tightened. After so many boys were born Pharaoh became suspicious and he ordered his soldiers to check every baby and throw the boys into the river as food for the crocodiles. Since then, the soldiers have been keeping a close eye on all pregnant women and there have been veritable raids in the area looking for newborn boys.

No wonder Jochebed is concerned. She stays indoors as much as possible, so the soldiers will not notice her pregnancy. As a result, Miriam must do a lot of chores outside the house which is also a great concern to Jochebed. Fortunately, the community pays close attention to each other and Miriam usually fetches water or goes to the market with one of the other women from their community. On one of those outings, Miriam sees the beautiful daughter of the pharaoh

—

bathing by the river. Like any young girl, she swoons away at the sight of a real princess, and she looks amazed at the beautiful ladies who accompany the princess. The contrast with her community is huge as they all live a very simple life. Miriam imagines how different life at court must be.

The day of her delivery has come. This time Shiphrah has taken her little ones with her when she visits Jochebed and her family. Miriam plays with the children as she listens to the muffled noises coming from their tiny house. Whenever a soldier passes by she must quickly warn Shiphrah so she can silence her mother. It is after sunset that the baby is finally born. Amram hears a soft baby cry when he comes home after a long exhausting day of work in the scorching sun. His heart is pounding, what will it be? Shiphrah says: "It is a boy: Ben Amram!" Only this time, there is no room for pride, and Amram kneels by his wife's bed and buries his head against her shoulder. Together they cry softly because they do not know what to do. Again, it is Shiphrah who comes with a solution: as Jochebed has stayed indoors for months, she should now stay indoors with her son. In the meantime, they will pray that the Almighty God will provide a solution so that the life of this young Hebrew boy will be spared.

It has been three nerve-racking months, but they managed to keep the soldiers away. Ben Amram is a quiet baby, so at first, his cry was not noticeable, but since he is growing older each day, keeping him quiet has become a challenge more and more. When Jochebed hears the soldiers coming closer to their house, her nerves are wrecking her. She can no longer stand the pressure. Something must be done quickly before the soldiers find Ben Amram. She screams out to the Almighty God as she prays day and night for a solution.

Then Miriam comes up with an idea, a very daring plan. Thinking of the princess's beauty, she shares her idea with her mother. A princess so beautiful can only be nice to a baby boy like her brother, she thinks. Initially, Amram and Jochebed are not very enthused about Miriam's plan, but gradually certain confidence comes over them. Could this be what they prayed for? A solution that they never dared to think of. Who knows, this might be the answer to their prayers.

That evening Amram is making a basket. He smears the inside with clay and then Jochebed places a thick blanket inside the basket. Then she put Ben Amram inside the basket. Tears run down her cheeks, but she knows this is the only solution. She entrusts her son to the Almighty and makes sure she stores the memories of this little boy carefully in her mind. Will she ever see him again? Will this basket become his death, or will it bring forth life? Together they send the basket to the river and place it between the caned riverbanks just before the princess's bathing time. Amram and Jochebed rush back to the house before the soldiers might spot them, but Miriam's curiosity has awakened, and she decides to stay around and wait for what will happen next.

As we all know, this story ends well. A real miracle takes place. The princess hears the cry of the baby and asks for the basket. When she sees the little boy inside, she instantly falls in love with him and wants to take him as her own. Miriam offers to find someone who could nurse the baby until he is old enough to live with the princess. Eventually, little Moses as the princess called him, returns to his mother. Every time Jochebed feeds the baby she thanks the Almighty for this great miracle. She is very sure that God has a special plan for Moses in the future. Her trust in the Eternal has not been betrayed.

*Narrated from Exodus 1:15-2:10*

## DISCUSSION

Put yourself in Moses' mother's place, could you do what she did? Are you able to give up your child for someone else to raise? Could you trust God so much that you would leave your newborn baby at a dangerous place near the riverside, hoping he would be saved?

## LIFE EXPERIENCE

When I am to start a long journey, most of the time I am not looking forward to the long-lasting, uncomfortable ride on the bus. I am quite tall, and my legs are always stuck between my chair and the chair in front of me. That is not very comfortable, and the roads are mostly unpaved, dusty, and bumpy, which makes a long journey very unpleasant. It can make me so moody in advance that every small, unexpected thing will make me go crazy.

Do you recognize that? Some circumstances are so overwhelming and all-consuming that you will lose perspective?

In some parts of Africa, it is a cultural habit to give up your first-born girl to be raised by a relative like your sister, your sister-in-law, or any other female relative. Habiba had to go through this cultural practice also. She had been carrying her baby girl for 9 months, only to give her up to her husband's junior sister. Who has been raising the girl as her own? Mother and daughter saw each other occasionally, but the sister-in-law, together with Habiba's husband, had final authority over the girl until she is an adult. Can you imagine the pain Habiba had to go through? Giving up her firstborn, leaving her empty-handed. She had become a mother, but she was not able to practice motherhood. What an impact this would have on her own life.

The purpose of this practice is that one cannot solely raise a child. It is the responsibility of the whole community to do so. Giving up your child like this shows that you are willing to share your upbringing with others. It is a form of trust. Trusting that other women in the community or family will take the responsibility of the child as Habiba would have done.

Though it was not an easy thing to go through, and it was not her own decision that made her give up her firstborn, in the end, she could accept it the way it was. The greater purpose is to uphold their cultural practice. And it needed to be kept alive. God's perspective was bigger though. The girl was placed into a Christian home and since her aunt was a Christian, she raised the girl as a Christian. When the little girl grew up, she went back to her mother's village and spread the word of God among the whole community.

God had a purpose for placing the girl into her aunt's care. Something, we humans, could not have thought about, but God saw it before we could. And he blessed the girl with the gift of sharing the gospel with her mother's family.

**Moses**

Jochebed means God's glory in Hebrew. Names were carefully chosen those days and often suited very well with the person. In Jochebed's case, the meaning of her name might have amazed her since there was little glory to be seen most of the time. Still, she dared to trust her God enough to give up her baby. Imagine what this means. Give up your child, loved by his mother who already had gone through so many difficulties, hoping for God to intervene. This requires a great deal of confidence, but it also shows us how desperate Jochebed was. I believe the plan to put Moses in a basket and place him at the riverbanks was inspired from Above, you cannot come up with this yourself. Moses is pulled from the water which is also the meaning of his name. He was pulled out of the water by Pharaoh's daughter, but, through that, the God of Israel pulled him out of the dire circumstances of their times. He did not do this without a reason, God's purpose for Moses was to become a rescuer himself many years later. God's perspective was way bigger than what Jochebed and Amram could have ever imagined!

**Letting go**

We like to hold on to things. Our jobs, our children, our partners, our families. It gives us certain security. In times of crisis, we find it very difficult to let go of our children, parents, or other loved ones. What if…? When we think of what Jochebed did to her three months old baby boy, it is inspiring. Trusting that God will protect and trusting in God's bigger plan for the future of her little boy. She trusts him so much that she places him at the riverbanks. Would we be able to do so? Would we be able to give up, sacrifice, what is dear to us?

# DISCUSSION

◊ Trusting God because there are no other options is quite conceivable, but what if the situation is not all that pressing and there are other options? Like in Habiba's story? Would you not choose the one option that suits you best? Even if it goes against God's plan.

◇　How do we know God's plan? Or should we be happy with sickness, poverty, and other terrible circumstances, because it teaches us to pray (and trust God)? How do you see this? How can we express our confidence in God during times when we are not so burdened?

## BIBLE STUDY

*You reached down from heaven, and you lifted me from deep in the ocean. You rescued me from enemies, who were hateful and too powerful for me. On the day disaster struck, they came and attacked, but you defended me. Psalm 18:16-17*

This psalm is a wonderful dramatic example of an emergency in which the psalmist cries out to the Lord (verse 6) and then the Lord descends to rescue him from that emergency. The poet uses the image of the ocean (water) from which God pulls him out and thereby saves him from the difficult situation and his enemies. This psalm is often quoted in the Old Testament (for example: by Jonah) to express self-help and the need for help. The beautiful thing about this psalm is that it starts with the dire situation the poet is in and from which God must rescue him. In the second part though, the poet has learned how to fight the enemy himself and it shows us a completely different image. The poet has changed his passive request into an active fight, and of this, we can take an example.

When looking back at Moses' life, we can see that he only could become a useful instrument in God's hands because a process of change had to take place. This process enabled him to become the leader of God's people. Rescued from the water as a baby, later in life he became an instrument for the salvation of many.

## DISCUSSION

Do you have moments in which the water reached your lips? At the time, what was a song or scripture that spoke to your heart? Share this, how did this work, and why this text/song? A song which always helped me was Psalm 18.

https://youtu.be/9wCTmn2TGjE

## IN-DEPTH STUDY (for leaders)

When you read verses 29-33 of Psalm 18 you might discover how to give praise to the Lord by pointing out all his strengths.

You help me defeat armies and capture cities.

Your way is perfect, Lord, and your word is correct.

You are a shield for those who run to you for help.

You alone are God!

Only you are a mighty rock.

You give me strength and guide me right.

You make my feet run as fast as those of a deer,

and you help me stand on the mountains.

The Psalm project composed a new version of Psalm 18. It shows us the phrase that he is a shelter, a shield, a fortress, and a deliverer. For whom? For those who trust in him!

Has trust then become a precondition for protection? I think this is what is meant: when you trust God, you dare to take up the challenge God has shown you or to do the assignment that he gave you (note, this certainly does not always have to be far away. Being faithful with our loved ones or work is equally important, if not the most). He will then surround you like a compound wall. Just like he did with Moses: because they trusted God so much, Jochebed and Amram placed their son at the riverbanks. Trust in God's care is most often the fundament on which missionaries dare to venture out into the world. The psalms are full of trusting God.

However, trust must grow, mostly by getting to know God more intimately. Scripture plays an important role in this. Through the Bible, we can get to know who God truly is. The longest psalm in the Bible (119) focuses entirely on the role of Scripture in our lives. It could be worth it to make a list of what Psalm 119 tells us about this and discover what the role of his Word could be in your life.

When doing this, consider the words 'law' and 'promise', because they are also parts of his Word. You may then conclude, like me, that knowing his Word and living up to his Word is crucial to the degree to which we trust God. It is interesting to know that the Hebrew dabar has two meanings: (1) 'to act' and (2) 'word'. So, words and deeds correlate.

## TIPS

1.  In difficult circumstances, pray to see God's perspective.

A well-known evangelist, Corrie ten Boom, once wrote a poem about weaving. She would show folks the underside of weaving, which was messy with all sorts of knots and crossed threads. You could not tell what it was or even see a hint of the true beauty of the piece. And when she turned it over, there was a lovely crown, beautifully woven out of all those messy threads from the underside. We often only see the underside, but God is the master weaver and will make something beautiful out of our lives if we allow him to.

*The Weaving*
*My life is but a weaving*
*Between my God and me.*
*I cannot choose the colours*
*He weaveth steadily.*

*Oft' times He weaveth sorrow*
*And I in foolish pride*
*Forget He sees the upper*
*And I the underside.*

*Not 'til the loom is silent*
*And the shuttles cease to fly*
*Will God unroll the canvas*
*And reveal the reason why.*

*The dark threads are as needful*
*In the weaver's skilful hand*
*As the threads of gold and silver*
*In the pattern He has planned*

*He knows, He loves, He cares*
*Nothing this truth can dim.*
*He gives the very best to those*
*Who leave the choice to Him.*

2. You Raise Me Up (song)

*https://youtu.be/gs2MoHbusac*

When I am down and, oh my soul, so weary
When troubles come and my heart burdened be
Then, I am still and wait here in the silence
Until You come and sit awhile with me.

You raise me up, so I can stand on mountains
You raise me up, to walk on stormy seas
I am strong when I am on your shoulders
You raise me up to more than I can be.

You raise me up to more than I can be.

# VALUABLE

# VALUABLE

# RUTH

## BIBLE STORY

This evening Boaz marries Ruth, and the air is filled with mystery. They are standing together beneath a sky of beautifully woven fabrics that depict them standing under the wings of the Highest as if they were in his presence. Naomi proudly lights the candles behind them. When the newlyweds walk by they receive blessings from neighbours and distant relatives.

The age difference completely disappears when their radiant faces turn to each other. "You belong to my side," Boaz whispers emotionally. "I will take care of you and protect you. Bethlehem will be your home and Israel will be your country. I will make sure that you and Naomi lack nothing. The difficult times you have been through will contrast with the happiness I shall give you." Ruth looks so happy when Naomi takes her hands and whispers, "You deserve this happiness dear. You chose to accompany me to my home and my people when you were going through a tough period. With this marriage, the Eternal shows that you belong here forever. You will be a mother to these people and I will enjoy the fruit of your womb."

Who would have dreamed this would happen when Naomi, Ruth, and Orpah, defeated by life in Moab, walked back to Naomi's native land? All three of them widows, Ruth and Orpah were still young and already so scarred by life. Their cheeks were sunken from malnourishment and with bags under their eyes from the long nights when they took turns watching over their sick husbands. There seems to be a curse on the house of Elimelech, Naomi's husband. The curse he must have taken from Bethlehem when he and his family fled from the famine. It had been foretold that unless the people adhere to the commandments of the Most High, there will be no crops, no fruit on the trees, animals will die, and no children being born. Elimelech thought he could escape from this curse by going to Moab, a neighbouring country where there was still food. However, in the long run, there was no blessing on the family there either. Even though Naomi's sons both married a Moabite woman, no descendants came and both young men died shortly after their father.

Naomi wished that her daughters-in-law would stay in Moab, because what does she have to offer them? A land where there is bound to be great enmity towards them for is not Moab the enemy? Isn't everyone in Moab living contrary to the Eternal's instructions? No, her daughters-in-law will certainly not be received well in Israel, so it would be better that they stayed in Moab. Orpah listened to Naomi's reasoning and decided to stay, but Ruth looked beyond her rational arguments. She saw a defeated woman, discouraged and bitter. A woman who might not even have bothered to walk back to Bethlehem, who might have neglected herself and collapsed in misery. A woman with whom Ruth has connected. Ruth felt sorry for her mother-in-law and decided to accompany her. Not only to take care of her but to become

—

a full part of Naomi's life, her country, and her faith. Ruth committed herself to Naomi's fate, she remained loyal to her and believed that together they will make it.

Indeed, it was not easy in this new country. They often had little to eat and huddled together in bed to keep warm. She remembers the long days in the field where she had to bend for hours to pick up the leftover corn. She remembers the moments that people were arching around her and started talking behind her back. These are the same people who are now giving wonderful blessings to her and her new husband. The women who first ignored her in the market are now crying out loud that she will have many children to make Naomi proud. For Ruth this is fine, she has forgiven them a long time ago. It does not occur to her to be bitter, since The Eternal has been so good to her and Naomi. Instead, she feels proud of the man who won her heart. She smiles as she thinks back at her mother-in-law's plan to give him the idea of proposing to her. Almost immediately after the first meeting, she knew that he liked her, although he still needed a little push to make it work. And that little push was just what Naomi needed to feel worth living again. What a pleasure she had when she told Ruth about her plan. The perfect way to be freed from adversity and poverty while ensuring the happiness of her daughter-in-law. Ruth's cheeks turn red when she thinks back at it. Tonight, she will gently remind her husband that this is not her first night with him. Our dear Naomi, who would have thought she would plan it that way, but it worked! The curse on the house of Elimelech is broken and from now on the light of the Eternal will shine on Naomi, Ruth, and Boaz, and through them, and many generations to come, Ruth is convinced about that.

*Narrated from the book of Ruth.*

—

## DISCUSSION

The story of Ruth is well known, but if you must compare yourselves to either one of them, would you be like Orpah or Ruth?

## LIFE EXPERIENCES

### African Marriages

Ruth had to cope with her new environment, culture, and religion in Judea, as we too experience this daily. Most of us belong to different tribes, with different cultures and practices. When entering the world of another tribe it is as if we do not belong there, as if we are strangers. We must adjust ourselves to their ways. This even becomes more prominent when we decide to marry a person from another tribe. Typically, it is the women who need to succumb to their husbands' tribal practices and religion. Similar as we see with Ruth. Only it was Ruth's own decision to accept Naomi's faith by accompanying her to her home country, but she too had to listen to what Naomi told her to secure a marriage with Boaz. Whether there was mutual love, was not important. It was Boaz's duty to marry Ruth to keep the bloodline going. Moreover, Boaz was a good catch. He was rich and he could financially secure Naomi's olden days.

Marriages are still done in this way. Love is often not the main reason for getting married. Financial security usually comes first, but the marriage could also protect a woman from undesirable male behaviour. And in addition, marriage gives women the opportunity to have children, something which is often not accepted outside marriage. Then, like with

Ruth, it is mostly our families who decide and approve which man to marry.

Some years ago, I, Renalda, came from a faraway country to stay in Africa. I was a stranger among all the others. It was not easy to let go of my own culture and traditions, but as time went by, I've gotten used to African life. I came alone as a single woman with one child from a previous marriage, but no husband. How do people find this strange in Africa! Also, the pressure to get married is high. Everybody tries to interfere with my personal life, and everybody knows an eligible party for me to marry. However, I think it is best to stay on my own until God shows me the right man to marry although being on my own without a life companion is not always very easy.

## Relationships

As the creation story shows, it becomes clear that our heavenly Father loves relationships. He created people to walk with and to talk with and share ideas with. Humans are designed to have relationships in all kinds of areas. A person is not complete on his own, and it will be difficult to reflect God's love. For that, we need each other.

When we look closer at the story of Ruth, we will discover that she has understood Naomi's need for her companionship since it is dangerous for Naomi to travel alone, being a woman at her age. However, Ruth's choice, through which she portrays a deep divine principle, also gives Naomi's life a special continuation and it plays a major role in the history of God's People.

The choice to stay with her mother-in-law becomes a different story when she says, "your people will be my people, your God will be my God". Their attachment goes far beyond ordinary worry, ordinary pity. This is a covenant between two women, a covenant that even breaks the curse between two countries. When we consider that the union between Boaz and Ruth first brings forth David and about a thousand years later, Jesus these words make Moab a part of the salvation of mankind! Ruth completely changes from her network, her social environment to that of Naomi's and thereby receives the identity that fits the people of Israel and Naomi's God. She becomes a child of the Most High and plays a part in the redemption not only of Naomi but of all mankind.

What I, Renalda, have learned over the years is that a life companion is not always found in a husband, but like Naomi and Ruth, it could easily be found in a very close friendship. This is more valuable to me than a marriage especially since an African marriage mostly comes with a lot of duties for the women and there is less friendship between the two parties. It is very unusual for a husband and wife to be close friends. I only wish to marry someone whom I am deeply connected with, and who is my best friend. So far I have not found somebody like this in this new country yet.

God also promises a close relationship with us. With Pentecost, he gave his spirit to accompany us through life. Even though sometimes I can feel very lonely, I know God's spirit is there within me to comfort me and to help find people to engage in relationships with.

—

# DISCUSSION

◈  Ruth and Naomi were both in need of companionship, which worked out very well for both. It brought Ruth closer to God. Who is your closest companion? And how does that manifest?

◈  We all know how it is to feel a stranger among other tribes. Even within our tribe being an only Christian can make us feel like a stranger. Or as a Christian within an Islamic region or country, we can easily feel as if we do not belong, strangers like Ruth. How do you think you could keep your faith in a non-Christian environment?

# BIBLE STUDY

*I pray that you may have your roots and foundation in love, so that you, together with all God's people, may have the power to understand how broad and long, how high, and deep, is Christ's love. Yes, may you come to know his love—although it can never be fully known—and so be filled with the very nature of God.* Ephesians 3:17b-19 (GNT)

Read Ephesians 3: 14-21 and think about how we, together with other believers of our Christian faith as well as other faiths, may discover the richness of the length, width, height, and depth of God's love. Paul describes an object where the dimensions represent perfect fullness. We can never grasp this alone therefore we need one another. By faith we may know Christ in our hearts, we belong to him forever but, we can only discover who he really is and how much he loves us if we too give ourselves selflessly to one another. Surrender yourselves to each other as Ruth surrendered herself to Naomi, to her people, and her God. In this way, she came to know God's faithfulness, his faith in her, and her faith in him. The depth of this covenant is expressed in the marriage to her redeemer Boaz through which she truly becomes one with God's people.

## DISCUSSION

◊    Do you trust God in a way that you can surrender everything to him?

◊    How do you express this? Surrender to God? Think about different ways which could express this even better.

◊    If you are studying this in a small group, talk about the ways your conversation partners are showing you the love of God. And how do you show that love to them?

## IN-DEPTH STUDY (for leaders)

*But the fruit of the Spirit is love, joy, peace, forbearance, kindness, goodness, faithfulness, gentleness, and self-control. Against such things there is no law. Galatians 5:22,23 (NIV)*

The book Ruth is short but special. Each year the Jews read it during the feast of weeks. This feast symbolizes the 50 days between Easter and Pentecost. On Easter, the Jewish people celebrate the journey out of Egypt, the deliverance from slavery by God. The 50 days following they wait while praying, singing, and praising God. They wait full of

—

anticipation of what is to come. Then it is Pentecost. A new harvest, a new beginning, and the start of new life with God.

The book of Ruth tells us about that. Naomi and Ruth start travelling, a new life ahead of them. A new country, a new house, working in the field, sharing in the new harvest a completely new life is waiting for them.

Ruth is originally from Moab. The Moabites worshipped many gods, but they did not know the God of Israel. For ten years she lived with her mother-in-law, Naomi, in Moab, in an Israelite family where she adopts their traditions and belief in God.

When it comes down to it, she radically chooses for the God of Israel and at the same time promises to be faithful to her mother-in-law, Naomi. The consequence is not only that her living conditions change, but she also changes personally! God's Holy Spirit is living in her. That is what Christians celebrate each year with Pentecost, that the Holy Spirit descended upon us. First, there is Ascension Day when Christians celebrate that Jesus ascended into Heaven. The people witnessing this departure might have thought they lost him. However, in his leaving Jesus gave a promise. In John 16 verse 18 it says that he will not leave them behind like an orphan. He assured them that his Holy Spirit will come in each one who asks. So, the Holy Spirit is not only visible in disciples, prophets, and kings, like so often stated in the Old Testament but now God promises to live in each one of his children. Men, women, children, white, black, healthy, or sick, God is accessible for everyone.

This short Bible book shows that God's character traits became visible in Ruth. Her spirit attaches to God and in this relation, she lives and makes choices. God's Spirit leads her and that changes her as a human. God's character traits, the fruit of his Spirit as Paul says in Galatians, become more visible. Love, joy, peace, patience, kindness, goodness, trust, meekness, and self-control. Beautiful traits of God, visible in us.

Ruth is a book of hope, peace, and a future perspective. She did not only make an enormous difference in her time but, through God's leadership, she had an influence that is still visible today. She is one of the grandmothers of Jesus.

## TIPS

1.    To whom can you be a Ruth or a companion? Or do you need a Ruth now? Let us pray about it and tell the Lord that you need a Ruth or want to be one yourself and ask for the right person to come along with whom you can spend time and strengthen each other. You will see that God will bless you!

2.    Let us be inspired by the following song:

> Everyone needs compassion
> A love that's never failing
> Let mercy fall on me
>
> Everyone needs forgiveness
> The kindness of a Saviour
> The hope of nations
>
> [Chorus:]

Saviour, he can move the mountains
My God is mighty to save
He is mighty to save
Forever Author of Salvation
He rose and conquered the grave
Jesus conquered the grave

So, take me as you find me
All my fears and failures
Fill my life again

I give my life to follow
Everything that I believe in
Now I surrender

[Chorus]

Shine your light and let the whole world see
We're singing for the glory of the risen King Jesus [8x]

https://youtu.be/uSl5KTc2D0o 

# Valuable

# MARY *the Mother of Jesus*

## BIBLE STORY

Mary is busy with the laundry, while her thoughts go back to last night when she walked around with Joseph in the coolness of the evening. They talked about the wedding which is about to take place and during their conversation they held each other's hands. It was a lovely evening, and she did not go to bed until long past sunset.

After the wedding, she will stay with Joseph's family and her future husband will take over his father's carpentry workshop. He has been working hard on making beautiful furniture, especially for her. Every night he is still working until she comes to fetch him for a short walk in Nazareth. Mary is happy! She is young, beautiful, and very content with her fiancé. And, although her family has little money and they live in an insignificant town, she is more than satisfied with the blessing that the Eternal One has bestowed upon her.

As she continues washing she thinks about all these things, until suddenly the atmosphere around her changes. It seems as if the sun increases its intensity, and a deathly silence appears. Surprised Mary looks around, but there is no one else in the compound. Suddenly she hears a voice and in a bright light she sees an enormous figure bending towards her, "Peace be with you Mary because the Most High is happy with you", Mary feels her heart pounding, what is happening here? Who is this? And why is the Most High happy with her?

Angel Gabriel, the one talking to her, says reassuringly: "Don't be afraid, the Eternal One is with you, he believes in you and gives you his blessing."

After this greeting the angel announces that she, Mary, was chosen from all the women among her people, to become the mother of God's son. No one has ever received a more important task, and no one will ever be able to live up to that. Mary, a humble, happy young woman from the unknown town of Nazareth, will go down in history as the most blessed of all women.

Not because she is better than all the other women around her, and neither because she is intelligent or sinless or from an important family. Only because her Creator has chosen to believe in her!

It took a while before Mary recovers from the shock. A few months later, while staying with her cousin Elisabeth, she answers the Most High's faith in her with a beautiful song of praise:

> "My heart praises the Lord,
> my soul is glad because of God my Saviour,
> for he has remembered me,
> his lowly servant!

—

From now on all people will call me happy, because
of the great things the Mighty God has done for me.

His name is holy; from one generation to another he
shows mercy to those who honour him.

He has stretched out his mighty arm
and scattered the proud with all their plans.

He has brought down mighty kings from their
thrones, and lifted up the lowly.

He has filled the hungry with good things,
and sent the rich away with empty hands.

He has kept the promise he made to our ancestors,
and has come to the help of his servant Israel.

He has remembered to show mercy to Abraham
and to all his descendants forever!"

*Narrated from Luke 1:26-56*

*( GNT)*

## DISCUSSION

◈    Have you ever heard God's voice?

◈    How do you hear his voice? And how does
it affect you?

◈    How do you know that God believes in you?

◈    What special calling or assignment do you think
God has given you?

# VALUABLE

## LIFE EXPERIENCE

When your parents or husband compliment you or tell you that you are very good at something and that they like what you are doing, it makes you grow inwardly. You feel warm and proud inside. It will boost your confidence and it will give you so much energy that it feels as if you can move mountains. A compliment or encouragement contributes to self-confidence.

In the northern parts of Ghana, where the following story took place, it is not so common to receive compliments. The best compliment you can get is something like, 'you have tried'. When you have cooked a nice meal for your husband, you will need to read his expression whether he likes your food or not. Fortunately, things are changing gradually, but many of us women have not received great expressions of love or encouragement during our childhood from our parents or our husbands during our marriage. Our parents were not used to this themselves, so they were unable to pass it on. They showed their love by working hard to provide for us, so we could have enough food to eat and clothes to wear, and if you were lucky they provided you with education. Wouldn't it make a huge difference if they had complimented you now and then? Telling you whenever you do something very well and that they do love you despite all the things that go wrong? Though our parents were not able to give us many compliments like that, we do know that our Heavenly Father does love us and cares for us and sometimes we even hear his voice like Mary did.

In the early ninety's madam Hawa was pregnant with her 5th child. Before she conceived, a certain pastor told her that she would become pregnant soon. However, Hawa did not believe the pastor since she was not familiar with prophecies. She was raised in the Roman Catholic church where there is not much room for people prophesying, but within a few weeks, she conceived. She was very happy and thanked God for this wonderful gift. One day, when she was in her third trimester her 5-year-old daughter said, "Mama you are going to die in December". Hawa was shocked. She did not understand what her daughter meant. So, she asked her, "What do you mean by mama is going to die in December? How come you know?" Her daughter responded, "Yes, you are going to die", and she laughed. Hawa did not know what to think, but when she reached the 8th month of pregnancy, it was nearing Christmas time, complications occurred in the pregnancy. She was taken to the hospital, where they realized that the baby had died in her womb, but the fetus was not willing to come out. The medical staff had to fight for Hawa's life. Many people prayed for her, and God blessed her with life; she recovered.

God believed in Hawa, and like with Mary, he also spoke to her. First through the pastor and the second time through her daughter. Knowing that something might happen, her husband sent her to the family to await the delivery. This was the best he could have done, as some of the family members had a medical background. So, when she went to the hospital, they made sure that she received the best medical care available at the time. God had spoken to her because he cared for her. And he blessed her with longer life. Though she grieved about the loss of her child, she felt God was holding her. He believed in her and let her live.

Just like Mary and madam Hawa, we all need someone to tell us that he believes in us, that we are valuable, and noticed. Someone who gives us more self-esteem by sharing positive words and encouragements, or a hand on our shoulders when we go through a difficult time, and who lifts us when we are down.

**Story of faith**

The Bible is a book full of stories about all kinds of faith, but there is one great story of faith that forms the base and is featured on every page of this special book. God's faith in his creation. His faith in the person he chooses to do something special for him. God's faith in his people, his faith in the church, and his faith in us!

God believed so much in Mary that he entrusted her with the most important mission ever. Her hymn reflects that great faith. The Bible is full of people in whom God believes. Abraham, Moses, David, Peter but also Ruth, Rachel, Lydia, and Dorcas. God decides to believe in a person, in people, and humanity. It was not their response to his faith that was leading, but his faithfulness. His faithfulness means that he has confidence in you and me and that changes the foundation of our lives. The word 'faithfulness' says it all, full of faith. he has a lot of faith, and he will not let you down.

Fundamentally it is not about our belief in him, nor our ability, our talents, or qualities, but it is about his faith in us. His choice for you as a person, as a mother or teacher, a seamstress, or whatever you are doing! It is about his faith in us even when we fail like the people in some of those Bible stories. Failing does not scare him at all, because he knows us inside out.

# DISCUSSION

◊   Remember the last time you received a compliment, please share this in the group (or write it down) and explain how it affected you.

◊   In addition, give examples of negative remarks others gave you. How did you feel about that?

◊   What have you learned from these insights?

◊   And how would you like to apply this in your daily life?

# BIBLE STUDY

*Even before the world was made, God had already chosen us to be his through our union with Christ, so that we would be holy and without fault before him. Because of his love God had already decided that through Jesus Christ he would make us his children - this was his pleasure and purpose. Let us praise God for his glorious grace, for the free gift he gave us in his dear Son! Eph. 1:4-6*

He believes in me! This is true, not only for Mary but for all of us; the apostle Paul assures us in Ephesians 1 that we have talents (verse 6). Here, Paul uses the same word that has been passed around to us from the message that the angel Gabriel brought to Mary. As the heavenly Father believed in the young and simple-hearted Mary, he too believes in you and me. He chose us to become his children even before the creation of the world. Why? Because he believes in his creation, a beautiful creation of which he says: It is very good! He has given all and everything to keep his creatures close to his heart. And because you are his creation, he sees you and he will be loyal to you. Every minute of every day he wants you to know that he believes in you and has faith in you. When you face difficulties, he encourages you to continue, and sometimes he will encourage you to pause or to fully enjoy when something special happens. He is involved and present in your life because you are his creation, and he is proud of that!

## DISCUSSION

◈ Do you experience that God believes in you?
If so, how?

◈ And what does this mean to you?
Do you find it difficult now, and why is this?

◈ How could you change that feeling?

## IN-DEPTH STUDY (for leaders)

When we zoom in on the words 'gracious' from Luke 1:28 and 'free gift' from Ephesians 1:6, which in Greek is *charitoó* and originates from the word *charis,* we do find the fundamentals of God's faith, his choice, his love for us; grace!

What is grace? What does it mean and how can you receive it? As Christians, we teach our children to say grace before taking food or before going to sleep. This way it refers to our prayer time with God, saying grace as in thanking God, but also, when a final invoice is due, you could ask for a deferral of payment and could be offered a day's *grace.* This kind of grace is more a granted leniency; the payment period extends by one day, but you still owe that money. What does grace mean to you? Have you ever thought about it? Do you refer to it only for giving thanks or do you also use it to beg for God's forgiveness? It can create fear because you might believe you owe God. Or does grace mean more than this to you, does it have a deeper meaning?

This in-depth study discusses a unique part of God's grace: he thinks you are an extraordinary person and that is why he chooses you! The word charitoó in Greek has multiple meanings such as, to make graceful i.e., charming, lovely, agreeable, to pursue with grace, to honour with blessings, highly favoured, gift, gratitude, thanks, and kindness.

The context of Ephesians 1 shows that this *grace,* or *gift* as we sometimes call it in modern language, has its origin in a one-time event: Jesus' sacrifice on the cross. This spiritual event in our earthly history has forever affected God's grace, pleasure, love, faith for and in us. Therefore, grace is not distributed like Santa does with his presents each year. Nor is it something we can rely on to get out of something. Grace is part of God's fundamental character and expresses itself in a loving and caring attitude towards us, made available through the cross. This attitude is formed in different ways and at different times, but its origin remains the same; God's election of his children even before he created the world. This was possible because Jesus bought us with his blood on the cross. What a gift!

## TIPS

1. Read Ephesians 1: 3-9 aloud as you glance at the mirror now and then. Relate the reading to yourself by replacing 'us' with 'me'. It could be useful to use the Good News Bible or The Message. Psalm 139: 1-16 fits in nicely with this.

2. Decide that from today onwards to only speak to and about yourself and your loved ones in positive terms. When you put in some effort, you will always find something nice to say including positive feedback. Remember the last time you had to correct someone, your child, someone at work, or your sports club. How did you go about that? Was it something like, "I see you, but maybe next time it would be good to…." or more like, "How many times do I have to tell you? I told you not to do it like that!" Practice positive communication in your mind or practice it with each other in the group. Keep in mind that God likes to talk to you like that too. Let it be something like this, I believe in you and in a great future that awaits you.

3. This is an old song, but so true. Great is his faith, his faithfulness. Which will never change.

> "Great is Thy faithfulness," O God my Father,
> There is no shadow of turning with Thee;
> Thou changest not, Thy compassions, they fail not
> As Thou hast been Thou forever wilt be.
>
> "Great is Thy faithfulness!" "Great is Thy faithfulness!"
> Morning by morning new mercies I see;
> All I have needed Thy hand hath provided—
> "Great is Thy faithfulness," Lord, unto me!
>
> Summer and winter, and springtime and harvest,
> Sun, moon, and stars in their courses above,
> Join with all nature in manifold witness
> To Thy great faithfulness, mercy, and love.

Pardon for sin and a peace that endureth,
Thine own dear presence to cheer and to guide.
Strength for today and bright hope for tomorrow,
Blessings all mine, with ten thousand beside!

*Thomas O. Chisholm-Text*
*William M. Runyan-Music*

https://youtu.be/2eQ1oal44wU

*To get more inspired listen to the following song . . .*

4.   https://youtu.be/-pZWCXFBVYA

# VALUABLE

# ANNA

## BIBLE STORY

This morning she woke up with a special feeling. The feeling that this is the day she has been living for her entire life. Anna has gone through a lot during her long life which was full of sorrow. Her husband died after seven years of marriage when she was still very young. Later she moved from a small village to Jerusalem to live with her oldest son. Despite being a widow at a young age, she never thought of remarrying. Her goal in life became 'the house of the Most High.' She visits the temple every day and stays there until late in the evening. In the morning she only takes a light breakfast, and mostly lives on what the priests give her. She does not need so much food, being in the presence of the Most High is more satisfying to her. For years she has been praying, fasting regularly, and praising the Eternal One. And over the years, her desire for a Saviour, the Messiah of Israel, has grown. She knows the scriptures. Even though she, being a girl, did not go to the Torah school, she knows the whole Torah by heart.

Especially the words about the coming Messiah have always intrigued her, the more time she spends in the house of the Most High, the more she longs for the Messiah, the

Saviour of her people. During the many years she spent in the temple, she has found people to be unreliable. Corruption, abuse of power, the priests, the Pharisees, the scribes are all guilty of exploiting the people who want to make a sacrifice in the temple. The building is refurbished on the outside, but the heart of the sacrificial service remained rotten. Anna keeps to her prayers and looks forward to that Someone who can lead her people back to the genuine values of life, true reconciliation, and finally peace for her city.

As a child, Anna learned from her grandfather and her parents that dedicating her life to the Most High is the most important thing a daughter of Jerusalem could devote herself to. Her ancestors were part of the small group who were left behind when all the others were exiled from Israel to Nineveh. In her early childhood, her grandfather taught her that only pure grace had saved her family. Hence, her family devoted themselves to the service of the Holy One of Israel. By naming her Anna, her parents declared they received her by the grace of the Eternal One.

This all makes her very sensitive to his spirit. So, this morning she noticed something is about to happen. She felt as if she is going to experience his presence today. All-day long she is alert, watching the activities in the temple. Then suddenly, she sees a small group of people. A young man and woman stand with Simeon, a man with whom Anna feels extremely comfortable, because, like herself, he too is a true servant of the Most High. She walks over to them. When coming closer she feels a tingling sensation going through her body. This is him; this is what she has been looking forward to for so long, this is the Messiah! Simeon holds the baby in his arms and lifts his head. With her arms in the air,

Anna joins the crowd and agrees to Simeon's hymn. It seems as if the Shekinah (the divine presence of God) suddenly descends on them. God's glory surrounds them, warmth and light that engulfs them, and everything in her life revolves around this moment. It happens right here in the house of the Most High in the city of peace where there has been a war for so long. It takes place within this small circle of expectant believers who honour the Eternal One for the baby bestowed upon this young couple.

*Narrated from Luke 2:22-40*

## DISCUSSION

◈   Have you ever felt God very close to you?
Have you felt his glory? How did you feel then?

◈   Did the church play a role in this or has to experience God nothing to do with the location (church building) you are in?

## LIFE EXPERIENCE

The House of the Lord, for one person a privilege to go to, for the other it can be an agony. Although the church serves a very different purpose than the temple in Anna's time, we still regularly call it 'House of the Lord'. It is the place where we together worship God, pray, and listen to what he has to say through Scriptures.

## Serving

In Anna's time, young widows were expected to remarry. However, older widows were encouraged to devote themselves to the Lord. Now, with Anna, this desire was there from a young age, and she could have inherited this from home. Her father's name, Fanuel, means 'the face of God' and gives a glimpse of the value of seeking his presence. The author Lucas emphasizes that Anna comes from the tribe of Asher. Centuries earlier, Jacob blessed his son, Asher, saying: 'Asher shall be a servant of kings.' And now Anna, a distant descendent of Asher, is serving the King of Kings, Jesus Christ.

Debra is a teenager when a pastor in the city took care of her. For over three years she lived in the church which at the time was a big tent in the backyard of one of the church members. When the evening came, she rolled out her mat and slept behind the stage, keeping watch over the sound equipment and other valuable items in the tent. Debra was present during every service, prayer meeting and choir rehearsal and her own prayer life developed. She was teaching Bible studies and started prophesying, so people called her pastor at a young age. The women in the church brought her food and she lived in and from the church, praying, fasting, and teaching the Word. When she got the opportunity to go to Bible College in South Africa, she took the chance, although with the hesitance of the pastor who had taken her in. Every year around Christmas, she would come back to the people she grew up with and share her knowledge. When she was about to go back for her third and final year of Bible School, she was convinced of the calling to plant churches in the North of Mozambique. But after one more year in South

Africa, a disaster happened: Debra died in an accident, as so many young people do in Mozambique. She is now in God's dwelling place, praising him eternally. What a great loss for the church in Mozambique!

## DISCUSSION

Living in the church, always in the presence of God. Both Anna and Debra did this. How do you practice church life and balance this with the daily duties in your house and work?

## BIBLE STUDY

*As soon as Solomon finished praying, fire came down from heaven and burned up the offerings. The Lord's dazzling glory then filled the temple, and the priests could not go in. When the crowd of people saw the fire and the Lord's glory, they knelt down and worshipped the Lord. They prayed: "The Lord is good, and his love never ends." 2 Chronicles 7:1-3*

After King Solomon built the first temple, we read that God's glory comes down in the shape of a cloud. This is the place where the people could consult the Lord, where sacrifices would be made to atone for the sins of the people. However, centuries later, the Babylonians destroyed this temple, because of idolatry in Israel. Later, a new temple is built under the direction of Nehemiah and Ezra, which was restored by King Herod in the time of Jesus. However, we do not read anything about the restoration of God's glory in the temple. When baby Jesus enters the temple, it is God himself who enters both his house and human history. God's glory has reappeared in the temple and, as with the first temple, this glory clashes with the idolatry of the moment at the temple cleansing, because of the corruption and abuse of the merchants, shows. Eventually, the House of God must be torn down again, which happened 70 years later.

## Church

Jesus calls his body the temple. With this, he has made clear that, if God's Spirit dwells in us, our body is his temple, his house. Paul builds further on that in the first letter to Corinthians. It is not a house or a building that makes holy, but the Spirit that has taken up residence in that house.

This applies to the church as well. The church building, however beautiful or expensive, is little more than a heap of stones or a bunch of branches. It is, however, the people who worship God in the building, which fill the house with God's glory by bringing his Spirit to live inside the building. In many cultures, it is customary to ask: where do you worship instead of where do you go to church? Worship: seek God's presence and determine your path from there. Our desire for salvation, reconciliation, to express love, and to let us comfort and encourage each other will all be done in God's house, a great place!

# DISCUSSION

The sanctity of the temple is an important subject in the Bible. No other God is to be worshipped but the God of Israel! And in the Old Testament, it must be done in a certain way. How is this nowadays?

◊  Where do you worship? And are you worshipping regularly? Do you enjoy it?

—

◊ Is the church you go to a place of worship for you? Or are there other aspects that predominate?

◊ Today there is much more room for influences from different religions and worldviews in our churches. How do you think this relates to your faith?

◊ Are the sacred precepts for the worship of Biblical times still present or is there room for culture-specific interpretation?

## IN-DEPTH STUDY (for leaders)

Psalm 84, of which the song is mentioned below, is an example of a psalm in which the poet expresses all his feelings and emotions about his love for the temple of God:

> *Lord, I cannot wait to enter your Temple. I am so excited! Every part of me cries out to be with the Living God. Psalm 84:2 (ERV)*

In this psalm, there is a fierce longing for being closer to God whereby body and soul cry out. It appears that, by going to God's house, the poet also expresses his longing and love for his Lord and King himself. One could compare it to a very serious form of homesickness that completely dominates the life of the poet. He only feels at home in the temple, in all other places he feels displaced. The psalm speaks of a pilgrimage to the temple as the Israelites used to do several times a year. The journey may go through difficult, arid places, but the poet is strengthened by the prospect of being with God in the end. That prospect serves as a source, an oasis in the desert, and gives him strength and comfort. Even though difficult parts of our journey should not be ignored, the goal offers hope which gives you the strength to continue. From strength to strength, from blessing to blessing!

## TIPS

1.    Your body is a temple for God's Spirit, it is the House of God. You inhabit the body together: Christ with his Spirit and you with your spirit. Now, who is in charge?

2.    What makes your body a sacred place? How can you take better care of that house, of which God has said it to be a temple of his spirit, a place where he can feel at home?

3.    Meditate on this song: Better is One Day

How lovely is Your dwelling place, O Lord Almighty
For my soul longs and even faints for You
For here my heart is satisfied within Your Presence
I sing beneath the shadow of Your wings

Better is one day in Your courts
Better is one day in Your house
Better is one day in Your courts
Than thousands elsewhere

One thing I ask and I would seek
To see Your beauty
To find You in the place Your Glory dwells

My heart and flesh cry out
For You the Living God
Your Spirit waters to my soul
I've tasted and I've seen

—

Come once again to me
I will draw near to You
I will draw near to You, to You

85

https://youtu.be/jdE03zRJtxw 

# VALUABLE

# Martha

## BIBLE STORY

She shifts a bit because her legs are cramping after sitting in the same position for this long, but she is not willing to get up for now. No, she does not want to miss anything the Master is saying. It is so wonderful that he is visiting them again after such a long time. And now that he is here, she is sitting right at his feet absorbing every word he is saying.

Mary is so occupied with listening to Jesus' words, she doesn't even notice that the house is filling up with more and more people. Her sister Martha regularly looks annoyed in her direction as she offers water to the followers of the Master. Cooking still needs to be done and with so many guests it will take hours. How can Mary just sit there listening? Doesn't she notice that she must get to help serve the guests? They cannot keep the guests waiting, can they? And they cannot send them away with an empty stomach. That is unthinkable. Something must be done now. Martha already has a plan in place, first, the goat must be slaughtered, bread must be baked and there may still be dates at the market. She sent a girl to look at the dates and tomatoes, but for preparing the goat meat she really must get Mary's help.

Martha slowly squeezes herself through the crowd. It is a bit embarrassing as she occasionally steps on people's toes. She mumbles apologies as she moves forward. The Master does not seem to notice her yet. Martha steps over someone who is lying on a mat, he is seriously ill. The people beside him wait patiently until the Master has time to pray for their sick brother. Martha wants the Master to know about this ill person because she would not want the man to throw up in her house or anything even worse to happen.

Martha is completely unaware of the story the Master is telling. He also does not seem to be aware of her. Even when she is right in front of him, he keeps talking. Mary is keeping her eyes on the Master when she suddenly hears her sister's voice.

"Master!", the voice is harsh and accusing, worse than Martha intended. The Master's eyes finally turn towards her. "What is it, Martha? Do you want to ask me something?" Martha takes a deep breath and, with an oblique look at Mary, she says, "Lord, don't you care that I am doing all the work alone and my sister is not helping me? Tell her to help me." The Master's eyes look at her warmly, the silence in the crowded room is becoming a bit uncomfortable. Mary looks around, suddenly aware of the problem. She has indeed left Martha alone. She takes Martha's hand, and pulls it, "Come and sit beside me", she whispers, "I'll help you with cooking later. The Master is telling such a wonderful story right now".

Martha hesitates for a moment but feels how the Master nods encouragingly. As if he were saying, "Come on, Martha, it's okay!" While she settles herself on the ground among the people, she still feels the Master's warm glance upon her. He says with a deep voice, "Only one thing is necessary. Mary

—

has chosen the best part, and it will not be taken away from her." A shiver runs through Martha's body, and despite the correction, she experiences a warm feeling. The meal will also be fine without the goat meat. At least the food will be ready a lot sooner, she thinks, while she focuses on the story of the Master.

*Narrated from Luke 10: 38-42*

## DISCUSSION

◊   Who do you recognize yourself in the most?
Mary or Martha and how does this show?

◊   What do you think is the main message of this story?

## LIFE EXPERIENCE

I, Laura, once visited my friends in Mozambique while there was a storm. Rain was pouring out of the sky and within no time the courtyard flooded. My friend, the mother of four and still carrying the youngest, was running around. Trying to save things from the garden, meanwhile fetching buckets full of water so they would have enough for the coming months for washing. The little boy on her back was crying loud and both were pouring wet. I felt deeply sorry for her and asked, "Where is your husband? Can't he help?" She replied, "He is praying."

What is better to do? At that moment, I failed to see that the husband had chosen the better part. It felt so unfair that my friend was running around, and the husband was nowhere to be seen. So, I do understand the feelings of Martha, looking

—

at Mary enjoying the stories of Jesus while there was so much work.

To me, it seems as if African women have so much energy. They get up around four in the morning, work all day, manage the household, go to the market, work in the fields, or work at their job in town. And at the same time, I notice my friend being zealous in praying and teaching the Word of God, although it is complicated for her to find the time.

Jesus said to Martha, 'Your sister has chosen the better part.' What about the work that is waiting? It is not going away and when visitors come, they do need food and accommodation. It is complicated to find a good balance between family, work, and church.

## DISCUSSION

◈ How do you manage your time with God?
   Are you satisfied with this?

◈ Is it possible in your family situation to divide
   the tasks so it is easier to have private time to
   worship and pray?

◈ It is said: living our life is worshipping God.
   How could doing our 'jobs' be combined with
   worshipping?

## BIBLE STUDY

*Jesus then said, "I am the one who raises the dead to life! Everyone who has faith in me will live, even if they die. And everyone who lives because of faith in me will never really die. Do you believe this?" "Yes, Lord!" she*

*replied. "I believe that you are Christ, the Son of God.
You are the one we hoped would come into the world."
John 11:25-27*

The story in John 11:1-44 shows us how Jesus cared for Martha and that she did hear his words. In verse 5 she is mentioned by name as someone whom Jesus loves very much. In this story, we read that Martha's brother, Lazarus, dies. Many people come to mourn. In those times and cultures, which is not much different from most African cultures, people came by when someone had died and donated money to make the funeral possible. The deceased was buried on the same day and then seven days of mourning began. During those seven days, the guests often stayed in the house to comfort the next of kin. Mourning and going to a funeral was so important that even studying the Word of God could be skipped. In Jewish thinking, it was believed that the human spirit took three days to detach from the body, so the third day was important.

Now that we know why Martha and Mary's home was so busy on the fourth day after the funeral, it is understandable that Martha does not patiently wait for Jesus to arrive. She walks towards him to tell him what happened. The name Lazarus (Eleazar in Hebrew) means, God helps, but according to her it is too late for that and therefore she would like to speak privately to Jesus. It is very interesting to see how Jesus takes his time to start a conversation with her (verses 21-26). Nowhere in this story, not at the beginning nor the end, is there any condemnation towards Martha for doing something wrong or for not yet fully understanding the situation? Jesus loves this woman and wants her to receive his words of Life. The verses that we read today are an important testimony to this.

Then, on the fourth (!) day, when Jesus performed a great miracle and raised Lazarus from the dead, he puts his own words into practice for Martha to see.

## DISCUSSION

This section shows how intimate Jesus' dealings with Martha were. She could ask him anything, he made time for her. For simple matters (Lord, my sister must help me) and for life questions.

◊ How is your relationship with Jesus?

◊ Do you let him investigate your heart and open your heart to him?

◊ Do you dare ask him questions? What questions do you have right now, share them and find out if there are others (or examples from the Bible) who are also struggling with such questions?

## IN-DEPTH STUDY (for leaders)

The story of Lazarus is important in the Gospel of John. It can be compared to presenting his business card which states, 'I am Lord of life and death.' At the same time, he shows the reason for Lazarus' disease, as he did earlier in John 9 when the disciples asked him the cause of someone's blindness. Jesus reveals that Lazarus' disease is not meant to be deadly, but to glorify God, to bring him honour, and to reveal who he is. The original words used in Scripture are the same in chapters 9 and 11, 'Through this disease, the glory of God must become visible.' It must culminate in revealing the identity of Jesus as the Son of God and his mission here on earth.

Verse 5 tells us that Jesus loves this family, there is an intimate association with all three although it is in different forms. Since the sisters have informed him of the seriousness of the situation, Jesus decides to return to Judea, an area where he was persecuted. This step to raise Lazarus from the dead seems to become the introduction to Jesus' death and resurrection.

The threat of persecution is why the disciples in verse 8 ask him why he wants to go back there. From this question, it could be said that they do not yet understand what is to come. They do not want Jesus to go back to the dangerous territory, because he could be killed. In this context, it is so wonderful that Jesus tries to open a woman's eyes to show who he is and through their conversation shows her what is to come. Several times Jesus tries to prepare his followers for what is going to happen. However, in this chapter, he especially takes Martha aside. He wants her to believe, to trust that he is Lord of life and death.

Just as in primary school now and then a student gets extra attention by receiving explanations from the teacher. Here Jesus explains to her especially and privately what he is going to do and confirms this by demonstrating it. The resurrection of Lazarus aims to get Jesus' disciples to believe (verse 15), not so much in his power but his identity. He is the Resurrection and the Life, even now!

# VALUABLE

## TIPS

1.    Think about when you want to take time for Jesus. That could be daily, weekly, or monthly whatever fits best in your daily activities. Try to set apart some time for Jesus. Go to a special place where you can be alone where nobody can disturb you and sit quietly at Jesus' feet. During this time, you could read from your Bible or pray or just be quiet to hear what God has to say to you.

2.    Make a prayer (diary) book. Take a notebook and during your time with God, you can write down the most beautiful verses you have read and your thoughts about them. We, women, are often very busy with daily activities in our heads. Writing down your prayers helps you to focus. Then the next time you have your quiet time you could start by looking back at what you previously wrote down. You will be amazed how God answers your prayers.

3.    Read more about Listening Prayers by Jim Harrison and how to put those into practice:

https://www.faithward.org/listening-prayer-hear-god/

4. Listen to the following song: The more I seek you, the more I find you from Kari Jobe:  *The more I seek you*

*The more I seek you*
*The more I find you, the more I love you*

*I wanna sit at your feet*
*Drink from the cup in your hand*
*Lay back against you and breath, feel your heartbeat*
*This love is so deep, it's more than I can stand*
*I melt in your peace, it's overwhelming*

*The more I seek you*
*The more I find you*
*The more I find you, the more I love you*

*I wanna sit at your feet*
*Drink from the cup in your hand*
*Lay back against you and breath, feel your heartbeat*
*This love is so deep, it's more than I can stand*
*I melt in your peace, it's overwhelming*

*I wanna sit at your feet*
*Drink from the cup in your hand*
*Lay back against you and breath, feel your heartbeat*
*This love is so deep, it's more than I can stand . . .*

https://youtu.be/NI_1YliutzA

# VALUABLE

## BIBLE STORY

While pulling and pushing she paves herself way through the crowd on the shore of the lake. She knows that being here will be a challenge. There is a good chance that she will be called names, be beaten, and be spit on. Yet, she is determined. She goes to the One who is her last hope for a cure. She sets off in her most beautiful and colourful dress decorated with gently tinkling bells. Then at the lakeside, she finds the One she is looking for.

For twelve years she has been suffering from chronic blood loss which has drastically changed her life. She is continuously considered unclean and therefore excluded from her community. Every day she feels lonely. She does not belong anywhere; she is an outcast with no future perspective. Her illness determines the course of her life whether she likes it or not.

She has tried everything to get well. After so many years of taking advice from healers, she knows more about plants and herbs than many herbalists from around the world. Healers and religious leaders can no longer fool her, she has long given up the belief in their remedies. She has paid large sums

—

of money to pretenders, priests, and so-called healers, who promised to heal her, but unfortunately, it has brought her nothing but pain, misery, and an empty pocket.

Then, she heard about Jesus, the special One. An inexplicable feeling has taken possession of her. She feels she must go to him. She knows that he is the only One who can heal her. She does not understand it herself, but she knows it for sure. This Man can make her better.

So, there she goes! When she arrives at the lakeside she sees him surrounded by a large crowd. She panics, how is she going to get close to him? Should she push people away to make her way? There is nothing else she can do. So, she starts pushing and pulling her way to the One who might be able to heal her.

"Hey, you, you unclean woman, you shouldn't be here! Get out! Go away!" She tries to avoid a punch and dodges an outstretched arm! With her arms in front of her face to avoid more punches, she pushes forward as much as possible. And suddenly, as if by a miracle, she is standing right in front of him.

He is a simple man. She almost pushed him aside, looking for the real Jesus. In her fantasy, he is like a mysterious, handsome, charismatic man, but Jesus turns out to have none of these qualities! And yet she feels an irrepressible urge to touch him. She is convinced that he is the One who can heal her. He and no one else!

Careful but firmly she reaches out to him. She tries to avoid a punch, but she is too late. "Go away, you unclean woman! You can't be here! You don't belong here! How dare you come here with your unclean body." She gets kicked and is spat right in the face. Humiliated. Left out. She is no longer welcome in the community where she was born. She no longer has a home. Simply because she has this terrible disease. In tears, but determined, she tries again. She stretches out her hand and this time it works. She can barely reach him, but she manages to touch the fringe of his cloth, and immediately she feels a deep warmth flowing through her lower abdomen. She is healed! She feels she is.

At the same time, Jesus turns around and looks at the crowd. "Who has touched me?", he asks. Shocked she hides behind a huge fisherman's back. She does not want to draw his attention, she wants to go, now!

Jesus searches the crowd to look for the one who touched him. She cannot ignore him, and she does not want to! Tripping over other people's feet, she falls to her knees right before him. 'It was I, Lord, it was I who touched you', and she confesses everything, her pain, her ailments, her search for a cure and he listens! At the end of her story, he looks at her with compassion. Daughter, your faith has saved you. Shalom, go in peace!

Narrated from Mark 5:25-34, Luke 8:43-48

## DISCUSSION

- ◊  Do you recognize anything of this story in your own life?
- ◊  How has that determined your life?

- ◊  Human connection can sometimes be complicated. Do you see a difference between the connection with Jesus and other people? What difference do you see or notice?

# Valuable

## LIFE EXPERIENCE

Napari is a young woman who suffered from epilepsy since childhood. She was brought up in a loving Muslim home and her family had done all they could to 'cure' her from this disease, but when they did not see any improvement they left her alone. Now, Napari is a grown woman seeking refuge in the church, the only place where people lend a helping hand.

Though she stays in the family compound she is not always welcome to join the others for food. They give her the impression that she is useless. Though her family does not believe she is an outcast, she is a pariah in her community. People do not value her as a person, they do not value her qualities and her abilities. Since the sickness has not been monitored by a proper neurologist, it has become worse over time and caused brain damage, which makes her behave differently from others. Even when she was offered the opportunity to join a program for young girls to learn a skill, she was not allowed to do it due to pressure from the other students and teachers. This is because the training institute might lose its good reputation by training an outcast. If the institute would allow her to follow the training course, they will suffer because other students would not be willing to apply for training there again. Now, Napari lives on the goodwill of the church and its members. It is a beggar's life with no prospects.

### Pariah

Being an outcast has huge implications for the whole community. It affects everybody and nobody wants to be associated with an outcast in any way since they might be looked down on as well. Everybody is careful not to associate with these people.

—

Being different from the others can make one strange, and sometimes it results in becoming a pariah. Many people believe these persons are of no use so they can do whatever they want to them, but of course, all in secrecy. What is not seen in the daylight, is accepted.

The bleeding woman was also a pariah to her community. People felt free to insult her, treat her badly, and do whatever they wanted to do to her because she was an outcast. Jesus too was different and his behaviour seemed odd: he had revolutionary ideas about gender roles, religion, and inclusive society.

Nevertheless, Jesus showed us the importance of an inclusive society by healing people who had been cast out because of their illness, such as the bleeding woman, the blind, and several lepers. Moreover, he also included those who were considered sinners by forgiving them and reminding them of their self-esteem, such as the adulterer and the Samaritan woman at the well. The people were not ready for this big change. Although they tolerated these uncommon ideas of Jesus, they disagreed, which in the end resulted in Jesus' persecution and death.

Today not much has changed. People who behave differently or have different ideas or believes are often discriminated against and sometimes cast out from society. Even within our Christian communities, it is not easy to accept people the way they are. Often women, disabled people, and other believers are disadvantaged in our families, communities, and churches, just because they are different. However, when Jesus was walking around on this earth he did not look at people's appearance, sickness, or convictions. He looked at them as human beings and treated them accordingly, by

—

including them as one of his and helping them to restore their place within their community. And, by believing and following him they became a member of God's family.

Today, Jesus' message remains the same for all of us. We too are valuable human beings, and he wishes to restore our places within our communities. Even when our communities do not accept us, we are aware that there is a place for us in his family where we can fully be ourselves.

## DISCUSSION

◈ Do you experience discrimination of being separated from your community in any way? How does it make you feel?

◈ Knowing that you take part in God's family, does it change the way you feel about being discriminated against or cast out? And if it does not change anything about your situation, how would you be able to cope with it?

◈ What valuable things do you think Jesus sees when he looks at you? How could you use these valuables? And how could you put these abilities into practice?

## BIBLE STUDY

*Jesus said to the woman, "You are now well because of your faith. May God give you peace! You are healed, and you will no longer be in pain." Mark 5:34*

The bleeding woman did not have a life. This woman must have suffered tremendously both physically and psychologically. The past 12 years would have had a terrible effect on her life and wellbeing. She must have been worn-out, sick of misery, and very lonely.

The psychological pains must have been even more than the actual physical suffering because there is nothing worse than living a life without other people. Exclusion by others by removing someone from the community causes serious symptoms of sadness and depression in the long run. People are not made to be alone. Jesus himself demonstrated how to share his life with others. In the New Testament, there are numerous examples where Jesus reaches out to other people and connects with them. Jesus shows that he wants to be involved, he wants to be part of our lives.

Connected with Jesus means that we may share in his Godly power. The bleeding woman sought Jesus' presence. She wanted to get to him as close as possible and she even touched him, because she felt that he alone embodied true love, strength, and healing. With whole her heart, body, and soul she was seriously looking for a connection with Jesus. Her hope was in him alone. She took a high risk by going out into the crowd, but she persisted and persevered despite the punches because she wanted to put her life in his hands.

That was what Jesus experienced when she touched him, and he did not ignore her. He placed her at the centre of his attention. It did not matter who or what she was. She was longing for him and that was enough!

Now she has transformed, from a quiet and withdrawn woman who kept herself hidden, to a woman who stands up for herself and who is bold enough to tell everyone about her encounter with Jesus and what he did for her.

# VALUABLE

And what did Jesus do? He took no credit for what he did to her, but instead he gives her all the credit she deserves. He praises her honesty, her openness, and her trust in him, and he even calls her his daughter. She is finally valued!

## DISCUSSION

◊ Do you remember your first encounter with Jesus? What was it like?

◊ Do you feel that being close to Jesus gives you strength and love?

◊ What difference does it make to you to be connected to Jesus? In what way does it help you to cope with your situation?

## IN-DEPTH STUDY (for leaders)

It is sometimes said that the Bible is like a love letter from God to men. God loves humanity, which is an act of his will. He does not look at what you do, what you have achieved, or what you look like. You are precious to him. In the book of Isaiah in the Old Testament, God says:

> *Can a woman forget her nursing child, that she should have no compassion on the son of her womb? Even these may forget, yet I will not forget you. Behold, I have engraved you on the palms of my hands. Isaiah 49:15-16a ESV*

God showed unconditional love to humanity by voluntarily choosing to live among men and to die for them. God loved the people of this world so much that he gave up his son

Jesus so that everyone who has faith in him will have eternal life and never really die (John 3:16). He is the supreme God and Creator of heaven and earth. He is Almighty and not surpassed by anyone. It was he who chose to become human and eventually die for us and overcome death.

Whenever I (Natascha) feel lonely, sick, or unwanted, experiencing God's unconditional love comforts me. I never feel completely abandoned because Jesus promised to always be there for me. Just like the bleeding woman I am allowed to come into his presence and tell him everything that burdens me. He promised to be there for me any time.

The book of Mark describes how the bleeding woman changes when she is truly seen by Jesus. Not only does she improve physically, but her behaviour also changed. From a quiet woman in the background, she opens and dares to share her story in public. Showing her vulnerability becomes her strength. She no longer allows others to chase her away or to intimidate her, because she knows she belongs, regardless of her status or origin.

Jesus himself says: "If you are tired from carrying heavy burdens, come to me and I will give you rest" (Matthew 11:28). "I have come to look for and to save people who are lost" (Luke 19:10).

## TIPS

1.　Do you recognize this? In situations in which you do not belong, you are excluded, people will gossip about you. You may even be called names or beaten. Try to share your experiences in the group. Recognizing each other's pain is comforting. You are not alone.

2.  Listening tip: Lauren Daigle, my revival:

*I will run and not grow weary*
*I will walk, I will not faint*
*I will soar on wings like eagles*
*find my rest in your everlasting name*
*you are my revival*
*Jesus on you I wait*
*and I'll lean on your promise*
*you will renew my strength*


https://youtu.be/lG7qn9Dx8xU

# VALUABLE

# VALUABLE

# Mary *the Sister of Martha*

## BIBLE STORY

It is celebration time! Many Judeans have come to Jerusalem because of the coming Passover. In Bethany, a dinner was prepared by Simon the Pharisee in honour of the Master. The people do not just come for him, but also for Lazarus who has come back from the dead. He is one of the guests, which makes Simons' house full. Martha helps Simon's servants, but it is so busy that it is almost impossible to greet everyone properly and offer water to wash the dirty feet. "Where is Mary?" Martha asks, "Wouldn't she come and help today? Where would she be this time?"

Mary is the family's scapegoat. Since the death of their parents, Mary has been off track for a while. She lived as if she could not accept that the three of them had to move on without their parents. It was so bad that Lazarus refused her entrance to their home for a while. As a prominent resident of Bethany, he could not allow her to defile his home. Martha never stopped visiting her sister, even when Mary was completely grounded. She was looking for comfort with every man in town and she did not care about what the people were saying about her. Until she met the Master. He immediately saw where her pain came from, and his words were like a balm for Mary's broken heart. Through Mary, her brother and sister also became friends with the Master, and since then he has been staying with them regularly when he is on his way to Jerusalem.

When visiting Lazarus' tomb, something special happens between Mary and the Master. Lazarus' coming back from the death brought immense joy, but Mary saw something in the Master's eyes that makes her think. She remembers all his stories and the explanations he gave, and today it suddenly hits her. She finally got it! Although he has performed the miracle of coming back from the dead, he will have to die at Passover. He is the Lamb to be slaughtered this year. This insight upsets her, and Mary looks for Martha to discuss it but Martha is too busy preparing for that evening's party and has no time for her. What should she do? This might be their last meal together. Mary does not hesitate for a second and goes to the room where she knows Lazarus keeps his money. She takes all the coins, wraps them in her cloth, and quickly makes her way to Jerusalem.

It is already dark when she returns from Jerusalem. The dinner has started, and people are enjoying the food. Mary hurries inside and looks for the Master. The guests observe her suspiciously. When she sees him, she rushes over and kneels at his feet. Immediately, her eyes are filled with tears as she considers what will happen in the days to come. She removes a small jar from her cloth and breaks it. A wonderful scent fills the room, and the air becomes heavy. The veil on her head falls but Mary does not notice it. Tears mingle with the lovely oil, and she rubs them on the Master's feet. She looks up to the Master and knows that he understands why she is doing this. She bows her head and kisses his feet. She wraps her arms around his legs and sits close to him like a little child who does not want her father to leave.

It is as if Martha is nailed to the ground. Also, Lazarus seems astonished by what he sees. Everyone is watching with wide eyes what is happening between the Master and Mary when a voice out of nowhere says, "Master, what a waste! Do you know how expensive this oil is? This money could have been better given to the poor". It was Judas who spoke. The other disciples mutter in agreement. Lazarus also nods but wonders where the money to buy this perfume came from. However, the Master looks around and answers, "Leave Mary alone! She has kept this perfume for my burial. You will always have the poor with you, but you won't always have me."

Simon then stands up and says, "Master, do you not know what she has done?" Jesus replies, "Have you ever noticed her? When I came into your home, you did not give me any water so I could wash my feet, but she has washed my feet with her tears and dried them with her hair. You did not greet me with a kiss, but from the time I came in, she has not stopped kissing my feet. You did not even pour olive oil on my head, but she has poured expensive perfume on my feet. She has done what you have failed to do because she not only believes in me but also loves me."

*Narrated from Luke 7:36-50 & John 12:1-11*

## DISCUSSION

◊ How do you prefer to express your love for Jesus?

◊ Are you exuberant or modest in this?

—

## LIFE EXPERIENCE

Although washing of feet does not often happen in most parts of the world it still happens regularly in Africa. Especially when there are long periods of drought, and the roads are very dusty. When we have a long journey, our feet often become dirty, and it is customary to wash the feet upon arrival. And even more often, the hostess offers guests the possibility to take their baths before eating together. Regularly, it is the woman of the house who provides soap and water for the guests to wash.

Hospitality is of vital importance throughout Africa. When we receive guests, they are warmly and extensively greeted. First, water will be offered to drink were after the greetings and further communication takes place. When someone is travelling and continues the next day, it is common for the person to spend the night before continuing his journey. After drinking water, people often eat together. All of this ensures that the visitor feels welcome. If a guest is not appreciated in this way, it is clear to the visitor that he is not very welcome.

**Hospitality**

In the story of Jesus' foot washing, the host failed to do certain customary duties to show his hospitality. Three special expressions of hospitality are mentioned that a host would have to perform during that time to welcome their guests. Simon had neglected to do all three. The first duty Jesus mentions is providing water for washing his feet which would be a welcome refreshment after walking the dusty roads. Mary, on the other hand, has performed this duty in her special way, by wetting Jesus' feet with her tears and drying them with her hair. A second special expression of hospitality was to give a welcoming kiss as a greeting. It was a sign of tribute and gratitude to the guest. Simon did not grant Jesus this act of respect. However, Mary has constantly kissed the feet of Jesus. As the third special duty of a host towards his guests, Jesus mentions anointing the head with oil. This was intended as a refreshment for the (dry) skin. Simon also withheld this extra token of hospitality from Jesus. However, Mary anointed Jesus' feet, not with the usual olive oil, but with an imported and very expensive perfume of myrrh.

For Mary, these three acts were not duties of hospitality. After all, Jesus was not her guest! For her, they were special tokens of worship and love.

At the Last Supper Jesus, himself washed the feet of his disciples and thereby declared them clean. After that, they were ready to enter his house. Since they were already at the table this does not mean that they actually would enter a house but this must be interpreted as a spiritual act. Jesus had the authority to declare them clean and to welcome them in his heavenly house.

**Burial**

In the Middle East, it was customary to anoint the diseased with oil. Before the Last Supper took place, Jesus' feet were anointed by Mary. This act can also be interpreted spiritually even though it happened then and there. He was anointed before his burial, an act of love and devotion prescribed by law. Paying homage to the dead was a very high priority in ancient Israel, and, although Jesus is still alive in this story, this honour was paid to him by a sinner. As if she sensed there would not be enough time for it before his burial. This

—

not only shows the restoration of Mary's honour but also that she was privileged. After Jesus' resurrection, it is this same Mary who he appears to first. She was a very loyal follower, and, in the early church, she was seen as an apostle.

**Forgiveness**

There are moments in our lives when we have gone very wrong. Sometimes we mess up so badly that we must humble ourselves before God to come near him again. It is difficult to clean up our mess, but when we do it, it is often a huge relief. It liberates us from the burden that we have been carrying. And at the same time, we feel grateful because we know that God has forgiven us. Forgiveness is the best thing a person can give and receive. It sets us free!

Mary knows what it is like to be forgiven. She was deeply troubled and was trapped within her sinful patterns. An encounter with the living God in the person of Jesus turned her life upside down. She opened herself to love, to receive, and to give. To perform what she did was necessary despite the gossip and misgivings of those around her. Much has been forgiven her and therefore she shows a lot of love it says in Luke 7:47.

## DISCUSSION

◊ Can you remember the last time you asked
 God for forgiveness?

◊ How did you feel afterwards?

◊ Did you notice a difference after you prayed,
 did you feel like you were forgiven?

◊ If not, what would help you to experience
 this feeling?

## BIBLE STUDY

*"So I tell you that all her sins are forgiven, and that is why she has shown great love. But anyone who has been forgiven for only a little will show only a little love". Luke 7:47*

Luke 7 tells the story of Mary. Here, Jesus makes it very clear that a person, like Simon the Pharisee who lives well, or at least believes he is living a good life, only needs little forgiveness. Given that he does not have to confess a lot, he does not need to receive much forgiveness. We could say that this is a very good thing, right? And we could easily recognize ourselves in him. Many of us have been raised as Christians and have always walked the straight, narrow path of obedience. As a result, our life with God is on a certain, steady level. We would not always recognize ourselves in people like Mary who did not always follow the rules of religion.

Whether you like it or not, there are people like Mary who still are, or have been, deeply troubled and who need much forgiveness. You could compare them to those whose lives have gone through a radical reformation process. Often these people might do things that people like Simon would find difficult to understand or even disapprove of. They could behave a little crazy in their relationship with Jesus. They show their love in extraordinary ways like dancing on the church stages, suddenly becoming a missionary, or going from house to house telling everyone the good news about Jesus and his love for them.

Yet, I would not like to encourage you to get in deep trouble first before getting to know Jesus as your saviour. When you fall deeply you might get damaged in a way that could not be easily repaired later in life.

## DISCUSSION

◈ However, what could be a way for the people like Simon to love more deeply?

◈ How could we further understand the depth of Jesus' sacrifice to grow our gratitude which would be reflected in our actions?

## IN-DEPTH STUDY (for leaders)

In Luke 7:41-42, Jesus used an example that connects forgiveness with showing love. This example considers the difference in the debt of both men. It is good to take note that even those with little debt still owed quite a sum of money to the investor. A piece of silver or denarii was equal to a day's wages which means that the person with the smallest debt still owed at least fifty days' wages.

The cancellation of the debt is linked, in the original text, to the word grace. It is by grace that both debtors are released from repayment, and personal merit does not play any role in the matter. For neither of them!

Then, when Jesus asks Simon who will love the investor more, we must connect this word 'love' to the word 'gratitude' which is related to grace. In this example, love becomes an expression of thankfulness for cancelling a great debt. The one who owes more will be more grateful. They will have more insight into what the lender had to sacrifice to be able to cancel the debt. Therein lies the secret. Awareness of sin or, in this example debt, plays a huge role in understanding the depth of Jesus' sacrifice. However, here it is not the cancelling of a debt that plays a part in Mary's behaviour, but God's grace. That is why Simon could still express his love to Jesus by showing gratitude for what he has done for him. Not just by forgiving, but for the other things God blessed him with.

Counting your blessings, one by one is a wonderful way to become more grateful and gain a better understanding of God's grace. That is why seriously ill people can look towards God with such great love and gratitude despite their suffering. The acknowledgement for every little moment causes a deep love for their Creator who never left their side.

## TIPS

1. In times you need forgiveness you could read Psalm 32 out loud. Confessing things that are not right in God's eyes is not easy, sometimes it is easier to just ignore your mistakes and bury them. However, also consider the consequences of not seeking forgiveness.

2. Think of a way to show your gratitude and your love for Jesus in a new way. Paint, craft, dance, sing, write, compose, give a present to someone, anything, but go beyond your boundaries and show him that you love him.

3. Read the article by clicking on the link below and answer the following questions for yourself:

- ◊ How has my life changed because of my relationship with Jesus?
- ◊ In what way can I be a messenger of the good news that Jesus is alive today?

Rising Up with Christ by Mimi Hadad

https://www.cbeinternational.org/resource/article/mutuality-blog-magazine/rising-christ

*To get inspired, read the following article by Elizabeth Garn.*

https://www.thegospelcoalition.org/article/what-women-need-to-know-about-being-image-bearers-of-god/

*To get inspired , listen to the following song: "I wash your feet with my tears".*

https://www.youtube.com/watch?v=aSWOkAGqtCg

# EPILOGUE

We, Laura, Natascha and Renalda have worked on this Bible study book for women with great pleasure and enthusiasm. It was an eye-opener to us that the long-distance and time differences could be bridged when using online media. Through this, we were able to cover thousands of kilometres with one click on the computer. We had online brainstorm sessions to decide which women stories we wanted to add to this study book. Renalda contributed from Ghana, Laura from Mozambique, and Natascha from the Netherlands. From our different backgrounds and experiences, we had interesting discussions on how to connect present-day African women to the biblical stories from the past.

It was amazing to discover that these biblical women were already confronted with life questions and problems that still exist among women around the world today. Thus, the Bible remains an incredibly present-day book, even though it was written by men who lived more than 2,000 years ago.

We delved into the lives of these biblical women, and while not much is known about most women, it was not difficult to imagine the feelings that must have been present, given the circumstances in which these women lived. Anger, fear, sadness, joy, these are emotions of all times and places. The situations and events are recognizable for all women from different backgrounds at all times.

It was even more surprising to discover that Jesus himself is timeless. He is very progressive because, contrary to the norm of that time, he places these common women with all their doubts and uncertainties in the centre of his attention. They preach the gospel and make Jesus known to people around them. Through all these stories, God sees women just as valuable as he sees men. He gives their lives meaning. She matters, without having to be perfect.

We got so excited about this first Bible study book that we have decided to continue with a sequel for there are many more biblical women in whom we find recognition, consolation, and strength. These in-depth studies will help to learn from these women and how to deal with the challenges of life.

**We would like to thank the people who helped make this book possible:**

◈ All African women who shared their stories, this is your book!

◈ Everyone who read along and participated in developing this project

◈ Our publisher Dr. Samuel Lee from SLWE Academy Press of Amsterdam

◈ timmyroland.com for design & layout

◈ The organization who supported us, not only in finances but also in hospitality and good conversations

# Valuable

# VALUABLE

# About the Authors

**Laura Gast**
Laura is mother of 5 daughters of which the youngest two come from Mozambique. She is married to Harrie and loves everything about different cultures (food, people, travels). She is the Dean of an international School of Theology in The Netherlands and trains pastors in several African countries. She loves to read books and chat with her daughters and friends.

**Natascha de Goey**
Natascha is a single woman with a warm heart for God and people. She loves her work as a district nurse. She also has a passion for speaking and writing blogs about her quests with God and his will for her life. In addition, she is creative, she likes to dance, go out with friends and travel the world. She has dedicated herself to this project with great passion for missions.

**Renalda Dijkhuizen**
Renalda is a single mum of an 11 year old boy who has a Ghanaian father. She has been traveling between The Netherlands and Ghana for the past 20 years. During her stays in Ghana she has worked at a missions hospital for 2 years and later she has set up an NGO to improve the economic position of northern Ghanaian women and to help spread the Good News among them. She loves Northern Ghana's culture, food and climate.

9 789079 516100